— **Praise for** *Believe and Rec[...]*

"Melissa Alvarez shows you how to integrate spiritual laws and principles into easy daily practice for immediate and long-term results. Stop struggling and start living!"

—Rosemary Ellen Guiley, author of *Guide to Psychic Power*

"A comprehensive yet easy to understand guidebook… Align your life with these forty spiritual principles and watch as your life spins from ordinary to exceptional. Keep this easy to follow reference guide close at hand."

—Della Temple, award-winning author of
Tame Your Inner Critic and *Walking in Grace with Grief*

"An inspired book brimming with practical application. Universal spiritual laws can work in our favor, or against us, and Melissa Alvarez shows us how to make them work for us, every time."

—Nathalie W. Herrman, author of *The Art of Good Habits*

BELIEVE
AND
RECEIVE

Photo by Isabel Barney

About the Author

Melissa Alvarez is a bestselling, award-winning author who has written ten books and nearly five hundred articles on self-help, spirituality, and wellness. As a professional intuitive coach, energy worker, spiritual advisor, medium, and animal communicator with over twenty-five years of experience, Melissa has helped thousands of people bring clarity, joy, and balance into their lives. Melissa teaches others how to connect with their own intuitive nature and how to work with frequency for spiritual growth. She has appeared on numerous radio shows as both a guest and host. Melissa is the author of *365 Ways to Raise Your Frequency, Your Psychic Self,* and *Animal Frequency.* Melissa's books have been translated into Romanian, Russian, Chinese, French, and Czech. She lives in Florida with her family, dogs, and horses. Visit her online at www.MelissaA.com and www.AnimalFrequency.com.

MELISSA ALVAREZ

AUTHOR OF 365 WAYS TO RAISE YOUR FREQUENCY

USE THE
40 LAWS *of* NATURE
TO ATTAIN YOUR DEEPEST DESIRES

BELIEVE AND RECEIVE

—— 🕊 ——

FIND *the* LAW
that WORKS *for* YOU

Llewellyn Publications
Woodbury, Minnesota

FIRST EDITION
First Printing, 2017

Book design by Bob Gaul
Cover design by Ellen Lawson
Editing by Laura Graves

Llewellyn Publications is a registered trademark of Llewellyn Worldwide Ltd.

Library of Congress Cataloging-in-Publication Data
   Names: Alvarez, Melissa, author.
   Title: Believe and receive: use the 40 laws of nature to attain your deepest
      desires / Melissa Alvarez, author of 365 Ways to Raise Your Frequency.
   Description: First Edition. | Woodbury: Llewellyn Worldwide, Ltd., 2017. |
      "Find the law that works for you." | Includes bibliographical references.
   Identifiers: LCCN 2017034513 (print) | LCCN 2017043157 (ebook) | ISBN
      9780738753294 (ebook) | ISBN 9780738751580 (alk. paper)
   Subjects: LCSH: Religious ethics. | Spiritual life. | Spirituality.
   Classification: LCC BJ1188 (ebook) | LCC BJ1188 .A48 2017 (print) | DDC
      205—dc23
   LC record available at https://lccn.loc.gov/2017034513

Llewellyn Publications
A Division of Llewellyn Worldwide Ltd.
2143 Wooddale Drive
Woodbury, MN 55125-2989
www.llewellyn.com

Printed in the United States of America

This book is dedicated to God and the Universal Energy within all that is for making me dig deep to discover how to deal with my abilities, understand spirituality, and giving me the courage, strength, and words to share what I've learned with others so their path will be easier to walk.

Contents

Contents

Acknowledgments

To my husband, Jorge, and my wonderful kids, Jordan, Jason, Justin, and Jorgie, for your love and belief in me. I love you all with all my heart.

To my parents, Warren and Nancy McDowell. You're the best, forever and always!

To Cassandra for support, guidance, and an in-depth understanding of the spiritual realm. Thank you for your patience when my clairaudience is turned down or I'm not paying attention.

To my acquisitions editor, Angela Wix, for considering a bunch of proposals at once, for answering questions, and for sharing in my excitement about my upcoming books.

To the staff of Llewellyn Worldwide, thanks for your hard work on my books, the amazing covers and ease of the publishing process. You're a pleasure to work with.

To my readers—you are the reason I keep writing books, you are my driving force. Thank you so much for writing to me and letting me know

Acknowledgments

how much my books have helped you as you've progressed along your spiritual path. Your input means the world to me. Thank you so much for being you, for reading my work, and for your support. Hugs!

List of Spiritual Laws

THE GOLDEN RULE: At its core, the Golden Rule is a natural law, also believed to be a moral truth, which states to only treat others in the same manner you want to be treated.

THE LAW OF DIVINE ONENESS: Everything you see and touch in the physical realm and everything you feel and experience in the spiritual realm are all connected and are part of a Divine whole.

THE LAW OF GRATITUDE: In order to get what you want in life, you have to be truly thankful for what you already have.

THE LAW OF LOVE: Love is one of the purest frequencies. You cannot see it, touch it, or contain it. You can only experience, observe, and feel its effects. With your heart filled with love you can reach the highest levels of spiritual awareness and growth.

THE LAW OF FREQUENCY: Pure energy is at the foundation of everything in existence and this energy vibrates at a frequency unique unto itself.

THE LAW OF INTENTION: The entire universe is made up of energy and information. It means utilizing this information with positive intention for your energy and purpose.

THE LAW OF ATTRACTION: What you put out into the universe will come back to you.

THE LAW OF ABUNDANCE: Everything and anything you can imagine is contained in the universe in unlimited amounts, of which you can partake.

THE LAW OF LIGHT: By transforming your consciousness and connecting to your own inner light, the light of the universe, and the light in one another, you'll open yourself to empowerment, knowledge, and a deeper connection to your own awakened consciousness.

THE LAW OF UNITY: We are all part of one spiritual being with each part working together for the whole even though the parts are different and unique.

THE LAW OF PURPOSE: Everything in existence was created with a purpose and has the ability to fulfill that purpose.

THE LAW OF HARMONY: Harmony relates to balance through energy. Everything within the universe is balanced. When you are connected to positive energy you will feel in harmony with the universe and balanced at a soul level.

THE LAW OF ACTION: Simply put, it means you have to *do* something in order to *achieve* something. You must take action to fulfill your dreams, your hopes and desires, and to obtain what you want out of life.

THE LAW OF AFFIRMATION: When you create a positive phrase filled with the intention of what you want, and you repeat the affirmation to yourself on a regular basis, then it will become your truth.

THE LAW OF CLARITY: If you are clear about what you want to achieve in life, have clear intentions, and clarity of purpose, then you can attain your desires.

THE LAW OF SUCCESS: You can reach any and all of your desired goals whether they are material, emotional, or spiritual.

THE LAW OF RELATIVITY: Everything in our physical world is made real by comparison or its relationship to something else. Everything is relative to one another.

THE LAW OF CORRESPONDENCE: The laws of the physical world which explain motion, light, vibration, and other scientific ideals have a corresponding law in the spiritual universe.

THE LAW OF COMPENSATION: You will be paid for the energy you have expended by receiving energy back from the universe tenfold.

THE LAW OF COOPERATION: As a spiritual being you are in cooperation with yourself, the Divine, and others in order to grow and learn on the earthly plane of existence. It means to make the best of what you're given without complaint or to take action to bring about change.

THE LAW OF PERSPECTIVE: Every person has a unique point of view or attitude when regarding something, someone, or a situation, which is relative to their personal belief. As belief changes, perspective changes. Life is how you perceive it.

THE LAW OF THOUGHT: Your state of mind, whether positive or negative, is reflected in your external reality. Thoughts are made of energy that can be targeted toward a specific outcome. This means to change your state of mind, is to change your reality.

THE LAW OF PASSIVITY: There are times in your life when you do not need to respond or take action, yet there are other times when taking an active role and making decisions is exactly what you need to do.

THE LAW OF SACRIFICE: In order to obtain something you want, you must lose, or let go of, something you currently have.

THE LAW OF RESPONSIBILITY: As spiritual beings we are to respond to the situations we find ourselves in and the people we encounter in an appropriate manner. To be responsible means to make our own decisions and act independently while being accountable for our actions without putting blame on others.

THE LAW OF ATTACHMENT AND DETACHMENT: You can have anything and everything you desire but when your happiness and sense of self-worth is dependent upon that thing then you are attached to it and must let it go, otherwise it controls you.

THE LAW OF FAITH: If you believe in something with strong conviction and trust that what you believe in will happen, then it will and the impossible will become reality.

THE LAW OF ATTENTION: Anything you put your attention on will manifest in your life. This is a simple law but is very important in achieving success and obtaining the things you want. When you give something your attention, especially your undivided focus, its energy grows and expands as it is drawn to you.

THE LAW OF FORGIVENESS: Is based in love and means releasing anger, resentment, hatred, bitterness, or other negative emotions you have towards someone or something; to pardon them for any wrongs done to you, whether known or unknown to them.

THE LAW OF REQUEST: If you need help you must ask for it, be ready to receive it, and should not offer help unless it is requested by another.

THE LAW OF ALLOWING: Trust in and allow the natural flow of life without resistance.

THE LAW OF DISCIPLINE: Doing what you know you must do even when you don't want to do it.

THE LAW OF CYCLES: The universe is made of energy that runs in currents, in cycles, ebbs and flows, vibrating at different rates at different times.

THE LAW OF PROSPERITY: When one person prospers, we all prosper in direct proportion to the happiness you feel for the other person's prosperity or your own.

THE LAW OF PATIENCE: All things will happen when the time is right for them to fulfill their purpose in your life.

THE LAW OF AWAKENING: In order to experience an awakening, whether spiritual, personal, or in any other aspect of your life, become more aware. To achieve awareness maintain self-control, stability, and focus.

THE LAW OF CAUSE AND EFFECT: Every action (cause) has a consequence (effect). Your thoughts, actions, and reactions (causes) create the consequences (effects), and these effects will physically manifest in your current reality.

THE LAW OF BALANCE AND POLARITY: There is a polarity between all things within the universe and between those extreme opposites you find balance.

THE LAW OF SUPPLY AND DEMAND: For every demand the universe will provide the supply to meet that demand, however, without a demand there will be no supply.

THE LAW OF POTENTIAL: There is an unlimited amount of possibilities and infinite potential within everyone and everything in the universe due to the connection of energy to universal consciousness.

Introduction

THE VASTNESS OF THE universe is filled with many wonders that are all interconnected and governed by natural laws that keep the universe functioning in smooth, organized, forward motion. These natural laws include both physical laws dealing with scientific studies and spiritual laws, which deal with spirituality, vibrational energy, and consciousness. We are each affected and governed by these natural laws, which are not independent of one another, but work together in harmony. In fact, we are an integral part of the universe and are interconnected to everything else within it. In *Believe and Receive* I am focusing on the spiritual aspects of natural laws and how you, as a spiritual being that is part of this universal energy, can use these laws to help you along your path.

Spiritually, you are one with all that is, all that has been, and all that will be. You are a fundamental part of the universe, of time and space, connected to its all-knowing consciousness, its energy, and intricate workings where physical reality is created. You will feel this connection at a soul level once you develop deeper connections with the essential universal laws and apply them to your daily life.

Are you tapped into your universal power? Do you remember the natural laws of the universe at a soul level? Do you feel at one with everything within the universe? Sometimes we all need reminders to get back to our core connection to all that is. It is my hope that *Believe and Receive* will serve as a reminder and a catalyst to reawaken your memory on a soul level. The universe wants you to get everything you ever wanted and obtain your heart's desires. The natural laws keep the universe functioning, making sure it has everything it needs to work, from the tiniest atom to the largest galaxy. Learning to use the natural laws will help you achieve everything you've ever wanted in life. When you're in harmony, balanced, and clear on your path; when you know the truth of the laws and of yourself, you can obtain everything you seek. The universe isn't going to simply hand you success on a silver platter though, it takes work on your part, but if you truly want something, and are willing to work with positive intention toward your goal, then you will achieve your desired results in time.

There may be times where it seems like you're not having success, even though you're trying your hardest, which can be frustrating or irritating. If you feel like this is happening to you, consider using a slightly different approach or give what you're doing more time to come to fruition. Sometimes what you're trying to achieve may not be in your best interest at that particular moment in your life. Don't think you're doing something wrong—you're probably doing everything correctly but the time isn't right for what you're trying to achieve. Sometimes you may have to put what you're reaching for on the back burner and let it go for a while to come back to it at another time. And that's perfectly okay.

Believe and Receive is a reference book that examines the natural laws of the universe through a realistic approach and practical application. The opening lines of each law (in italics under the law's name) can be used as a daily affirmation. You can repeat these affirmations to yourself first thing in the morning to get your day started and use them throughout the day for a boost in your frequency or to feel positive empowerment. I don't expect you to memorize every one of these laws, nor do I expect you to try to put all these laws into use at one time. That would be very overwhelming. Instead, use this book to refer to the laws as often as needed. You can choose to work with laws that have meaning to your current situation or select a law that you'd like to put to use in your life. Start with one and when you feel that one is working well for you, move on to another one.

While manifestation using the Law of Attraction is a very popular and potent part of the process, it works together with the rest of the natural laws and is only one law among many. There are literally hundreds of natural laws that will help you reach your goals. In *Believe and Receive* I address forty of them. I tried to select laws that I feel are very beneficial to soul growth and living a successful, abundant life. I also selected laws that may not be as well known as some popular laws. The forty laws included in *Believe and Receive* met these criteria and have been helpful to me so I chose them for inclusion. My purpose is to help you find the law that works for you through explanations that will elevate your understanding of the law, sharing my own beliefs and experiences of how the laws have worked for me, and by giving you practical tips for daily applications you can use in your own life. I believe it's easier to learn through examples instead of having someone tell you to do *this* or do *that* to achieve results, so this book is very conversational in tone. It's written to urge you to think, to consider new angles, and to take action when you feel a connection to the natural law that will help you on your own path.

I have also included the origin of the law whenever it is known. In many cases the law was passed down from word of mouth and an exact origin isn't known. If that's the case, I point out other places where the law is used or similarities between the law and other similar concepts. You'll find that four of the laws stem from *The Kybalion,* so I would like to explain it here. *The Kybalion* is described by its authors as a "collection of maxims, axioms, and precepts" that were handed down by word of mouth throughout the centuries until organized in written form in 1908 by Three Initiates, author(s) who wanted to remain anonymous. *The Kybalion* is based on the teachings of Hermes Trismegistus, an archetypal figure from the second and third centuries CE based on the Greek god Hermes and the Egyptian god Thoth.

Working with the natural laws of the universe will bring about changes in the way you look at and react to situations in your life, and it will instill a positive mental attitude within you. The natural laws enable you to learn to see the positive possibilities in everything instead of assuming the worst or looking at the negative, allowing you to feel and be one with all existence, to understand you are part of universal power. In everything you do, every person you meet, every action you take, there are lessons and opportunities presented to you. Learn to recognize them and grow from them. The greatest spiritual growth comes from owning these experiences and lessons, making them an integral part of your being, and moving forward in positivity because of the experience.

It's important to remember that to be happy with your life with all the things you may want to achieve, you must first be happy with yourself at a soul level. You have to know and love the real you, feel confident in the truth of your nature, and reach out to attain your goals. Happiness comes from within, from connecting to the truth of self, from knowing that, regardless of what happens, you will always be happy and content just being you. If you understand that material items will not make you happy but will enhance the happiness you already feel, then, when you achieve your greatest desires, the success will be that much sweeter.

There are six important things to remember as you walk this path:

1. *You are responsible for your own energy.* It is your job to make sure you're connecting with your own spiritual frequency and that your thoughts, emotions, and actions are in tune with

positivity, joy, and abundance. If you're out of balance due to negativity, try to bring yourself back into balance through internal analysis, understanding, and connecting to your Divine self.

2. *Whatever you strive to attain in life is also striving to come to you.* The things you want to achieve in life are trying their best to get to you. If you're reaching out for it, it's reaching back, trying to grasp your hand. When you're connected to your universal power, you're able to grab hold tightly to what you want and never let it go. If you're seeking more joy and happiness, know that joy and happiness are seeking you. These traits want to be ingrained within you if you want them to be part of your internal spiritual essence.

3. *The deepest connections with the universe are made when you take the time to be at one with the natural world.* Just spending time outside feeling the ground beneath your feet, the sun on your face, the rain against your skin, or the night surrounding you will give you this connection as long as you feel the stillness of the moment and interact with nature's energy.

4. *Be present in the moments of your life.* Everyone is so busy these days. When you take the time to truly be present and appreciate what you experience on a daily basis, you will deepen your relationship with the universe and natural law.

5. *Love is an integral part of the whole.* While there are many occasions where you need time alone to work on your own spirituality, there are just as many times where other people open your eyes to new concepts and ideas. When you create loving, positive, and honest relationships with other people, you are growing your universal connection. Just as you are an integral part of the interconnectedness of the universe, so is every other person. Every animal, plant, body of water, everything you see,

hear, and encounter is all part of the whole. Try to walk your path with others and with love for everyone and everything you encounter in life.

6. *When you look for the positives in life, you'll be filled with a sense of peace, and will experience less worry, struggle, and conflict.* There are times in everyone's life when we have negative experiences—that's human nature and part of spiritual growth. You will go through difficulties in order to learn life lessons. However, that is different from allowing yourself to be enveloped in negativity where you're always seeing the bad instead of the good, always procrastinating instead of just doing the work that needs to be done, complaining instead of praising, discussing the bad things that happen instead of talking about the good you want to come out of the situation. Sometimes you just have to get things off your chest; if you tell someone about an experience you had that is negative, just remember to also tell them the positives you've learned from the experience. Negative thoughts can serve the purpose of cueing you in to things that you need to pay attention to instead of avoiding it. Negativity is something that needs to be worked through instead of repressing, ignoring, or burying it deep inside. When you acknowledge and work though it, you will be able to release it so that it doesn't come back to bother you again in the future.

I want you to be successful, to see your dreams become reality. I want you to soar! If you open your heart and spread your wings, you can elevate yourself to the greatest heights imaginable. You can do it! I have faith in your belief in yourself, your desire to achieve difficult goals, and your ability to see the path through to the end. I know you're not going to give up because you truly want to obtain the things you need and want in life. Use the natural laws to ask the universe for what you want, work steadily toward that goal, and eventually it will come to you. To obtain a new result, you must walk a new path. Change is an important part of getting what you want.

Now is the time to embrace your universal power. Recognize that your thoughts, feelings, beliefs, attitude, and expectations are all integral parts of your core essence that, when combined and focused with positive energy and working through any negative energy, will allow you to be all you ever wanted to be and achieve all you've ever wanted to achieve. Now is the time to learn how to find the natural laws that will work for you in any given situation. Most importantly, enjoy the journey as you grow into your own awesomeness by becoming one with your universal power.

1

THE GOLDEN RULE

*Today I leave negativity behind and
will go out of my way to share the goodness
in my heart with everyone I encounter.*

THE GOLDEN RULE IS considered an ethical tradition. This means that groups of people, from nearly every culture and religion, believe that a concept or action is morally right or wrong because other people have held the same belief for a long period of time, sometimes thousands of years. The Golden Rule is a natural law that is also believed to be a moral truth stating to treat others in the same manner you want to be treated. Many ethical groups and religions have some version of the Golden Rule within their belief system. For example, in Christianity the Golden Rule is quoted in Luke 6:31, King James Version as, "And as ye would that men should do to you, do ye also to them likewise," and in Buddhism it is quoted in the Udānavarga 5:18 as, "Hurt not others in ways that you yourself would find hurtful."

To apply the Golden Rule, you must put yourself in the other person's shoes and think before you act or react. When you consider how your actions will affect another person then you see the situation from a different point of view. Actions based in love and harmony will allow you to be one with the Golden Rule.

Implementing the Golden Rule

So how can the Golden Rule work for you? If you're applying the Golden Rule, then you can bring about great changes in your life, especially if you've been previously unaware of how your actions were affecting others.

A while back an elderly woman was looking for an address for an event she was attending. She saw me and asked directions, but I wasn't sure exactly where it was. I told her approximately where it might be and she went on her way. About fifteen minutes later I saw her car parked at the end of the road. The event had already started by then so I went inside, looked up what I remembered of the address online, and had her follow me. When we arrived, she came over and gave me a hug through my truck window as she said thank you. I went home with a big smile on my face because I'd been able to help her. I could have ignored the situation but when I looked down the road and saw her vehicle, I thought about how I would feel if I couldn't find my way and was missing a big event because no one was answering the phone to give me directions. Putting myself in her shoes and knowing I'd want someone to help me if they could spurred me to act. Sometimes following the Golden Rule means going out of your way to treat people the way you want to be treated, but it makes you feel so good when you do.

Consistency without Conditions

The Golden Rule asks you to be consistent in your actions, which should be in harmony with your core moral code of ethics. For me it means treating others with fairness, kindness, and never wishing upon others something I wouldn't also wish for myself. Living by the Golden Rule means to look at the success of others as your own success and to be as happy for them as you would be if you had made the same accomplishment. Jealousy, hatred, and envy have no place when living in alignment with the Golden Rule. These traits will only cause conflict, where the Golden Rule will allow you to resolve differences.

The Golden Rule governs conduct and empathizing with others without conditions. One of my primary life rules is that I'll never ask someone to do something I'm not willing to do myself. When I was a retail manager, I'd clean toilets and climb ladders to change light bulbs and dust fixtures. Because I was willing to do anything I asked of my employees, they were more than willing to jump in and do the jobs, often without being asked. Once there were six of us on our hands and knees scrubbing the grout of the store's tile floor by hand. When it was finished, we all had a sense of pride for a job well done and a floor that sparkled!

When you live with love for everyone and everything in your heart, following the Golden Rule is easy. There's no stress involved because it radiates from within and is an integral part of your soul essence. When you treat people how you'd like to be treated, the universe in turn brings more positivity into your life.

If you encounter negativity when you're living the Golden Rule, try to work through it. If someone wants to start an argument or draw you into their drama, you can choose not to engage, participate, or retaliate against them (this includes online arguments on social media), but instead you can choose to leave the situation. You simply have to make the decision and do it. It can be trying at times, especially if they've angered you. Living the Golden Rule doesn't mean allowing others to walk all over you or take advantage of your kindness. Live with your eyes wide open, live by what is true and right for your own spiritual being, and know you can stand up for yourself and still treat others with respect and kindness. Living by the Golden Rule is your choice, just as it's your choice how you decide to handle negative situations in order to work through and release them.

Follow Through with Action

Giving the Golden Rule lip service and not following through with action can mean your motivation is in the wrong place, which can make life tedious and stressful. It isn't about keeping score to see who can do more good deeds; it's not about mentally putting conditions on another person so that if they act in a certain way, you'll respond in a specific way. It is about being so comfortable and happy within your own skin that you want everyone else to feel the same kind of happiness so you treat them with kindness, understanding, and most of all, love.

None of us is perfect so it's important that we don't judge one another. The young woman using an electric cart in a retail store may have debilitating arthritis or some other medical condition. You wouldn't know this about her. Instead of thinking she's lazy, send her love that she can overcome whatever ails her. No one can ever know what another person is going through. If someone is short with you, try not to get angry and act the same way. Maybe they just lost someone they loved, or received bad news, or were laid off from their job. Always try to take the high road and treat everyone the best you can.

Deep inside we're all the same, we all have fears, dreams, ambitions, and goals. We all love and want to be loved in return. We want to fit in with society, have friends, and engage in fun activities with others to bring us joy. We want good jobs and entertaining hobbies. We all want to be listened to and feel that our opinions matter. Take the time to truly listen to what someone else has to say. Try not to negate another person's worries or experiences; that's not living the Golden Rule, which can fill your heart with love, peace, and forgiveness. Most of all we want to be treated with respect, understanding, and kindness. We don't want to be bullied, ridiculed, or made to feel ashamed, embarrassed, or belittled.

Once you start putting the Golden Rule into action, you'll realize how your actions are positively affecting others and you'll begin to feel an internal transformation. You'll notice you feel better about yourself, more joyful and upbeat, because you're making a difference in other people's lives. You're looking for the goodness in others even when they're putting on a negative façade. You'll begin to look deeper, to the soul level, leading to your own soul growth. You'll find it becomes easier to trust others instead of looking for ulterior motives. The Golden Rule may not resolve every issue but it's a wonderful place to start.

Try It Now

As you go about your day, do the unexpected for other people. Hold a door open for someone, let the person behind you go ahead of you in line at the store, and greet someone you don't know with a kind word. Pick up the phone and call someone just to let them know that you're thinking about them and wanted to see how they are doing. These little acts of kindness go a long way in implementing the Golden Rule. Remember to apply the Golden Rule to how you treat yourself. It's easy to forget to treat yourself well when you're busy doing for others, but make sure you are as good to yourself as you are to them. You're just as important as everyone else.

Practical Application Tips

- A smile often helps a stressful situation.

- Treating others how you'd like to be treated allows them to feel your kindness and pay it forward to someone else.

- Every person deserves respect, kindness, and understanding, even a random stranger you encounter while shopping that you'll never meet again.

- Try to leave every situation better than you found it.

- Take positive action without telling everyone what you're doing. There is power in silence.

- Be compassionate and understanding in every interaction with others.

- Try not to engage in arguments. The other person may simply be having a bad day.

- Don't make mountains out of molehills when interacting with another person. Be respectful and you'll often receive respect in return.

- When you do good deeds that help others, then you will receive goodness in return. But negative actions will bring negativity back to you. Always err on the side of goodness for the person you're interacting with and so you receive goodness in return from others. This doesn't mean that you should be self-sacrificing. You must take care of yourself too.

See also Chapter 4: The Law of Love

2

THE LAW OF
DIVINE ONENESS

—🕊—

Today I choose to see my world as an integral
part of the whole. Everyone and everything I
encounter is Divine and one with all of creation
and I will engage with them accordingly.

THE LAW OF DIVINE Oneness states that everything you see and touch in the physical realm, and everything you feel and experience in the spiritual realm, are all connected and are part of the Divine whole. Every person is connected to one another, to every fiber of the universe, to God, the spiritual world, and the energy (frequency) that vibrates within every aspect of the Divine. This Divinity goes by many names depending upon your religious and spiritual beliefs. For example, in Taoism, the Law of Divine Oneness is the same as the concept of Tao. It means your actions and reactions, words, beliefs, and fears will affect how you treat yourself and will also affect other people, the earthly plane, and the whole of Divinity.

Physically we are all different; spiritually we are all the same. We may express different beliefs, but we are all made of energy and we have all chosen to incarnate on the earthly plane to experience soul growth. If we look at someone and only see their physical self and not their spiritual self then we're overlooking the Law of Divine Oneness. When you can view a person who is opposite from you in appearance, beliefs, and ideals and see them at a soul level, you are in tune with the Law of Divine Oneness. Situations where you must step out of your comfort zone often provide you with the greatest lessons and the most soul growth toward Oneness through love and peacefulness

Defining Yourself

How do you define yourself? Do you first think of yourself as Spirit, a being of powerful energy and unlimited knowledge, who is filled with the positivity of the spiritual realm and connected to all that is? Or do you think about what you look like, your gender, the color of your hair or skin, the place you live, your friends, and how you fit into society? The physical you could not exist without the spiritual you. It is within your core essence to recognize the oneness of being you share with every other living person. As you become more aware of the scope of the Law of Divine Oneness you'll begin to see fewer differences between yourself and others. In turn, you will look at the world with loving eyes instead of seeing everything and everyone as separate from the whole.

Have you ever seen a photo mosaic? From a distance, it looks like a normal picture but when you look closely, you discover it is made up of thousands of tiny pictures of individual people. Think of the photo as the universe and all the individual people who make up the photo mosaic as the Divine. If any of the individual pictures were missing from the whole, there would be gaps in the picture, missing pieces of Divine

Oneness. The Divine never has missing pieces. Every person and thing in existence is part of the oneness of universal Divinity.

Being part of Divine Oneness means you're never alone. You're surrounded by others whose light is just as bright as your own and each person shines with love. When you're feeling lonely, take a moment to think of how another's light has positively affected you and you'll find the loneliness will fade.

Become Part of the Whole

Let's imagine the universe as a huge lake. Every drop of rain that falls into the lake is part of the whole, yet each creates its own ripple in the water. They are unique yet in harmonious one with the whole. The ripples simply interact for a moment and then continue along their path, growing and expanding until they are completely integrated into the whole of the lake's water. Think of people as the raindrops, each with its own individual characteristics (ripples) that encounter the characteristics of others. There is no fear of these differences. They are just accepted.

The Law of Divine Oneness urges you to choose to acknowledge and accept the differences in others instead of creating fear based conflict or drama. When we all strive to be the best we can be, and lift up those around us to achieve their own inner greatness, then we're making the universe a better place. Let's go back to the lake for a minute. If there is conflict stirring underneath the surface, then that calm lake might suddenly develop a sinkhole in its foundation, sucking everything in its path down into its depths, even trees from nearby land. If you allow it, negativity can do the same to you. When you are critical or fearful of the differences of others, then you're creating a sink hole that can be very difficult to get out of. To avoid and not repress negativity, look at yourself and everyone in the world as Divine.

Making a Choice

When I was in college, I often found myself surrounded by people who gossiped about the differences in others. I didn't see the point. To me, what other people did was their business, not mine. I was having a hard enough time trying to figure out my own intuitive nature back in those days. Eventually, I stopped hanging around the gossips. This was a valuable lesson about the Law of Divine Oneness and accepting others as they are instead of trying to make them fit into a mold. Looking back, I can see their actions were based on fear, jealousy, and the desire to control others. In today's world you'll often encounter this same type of situation, especially on social media sites. There's nothing wrong with cutting ties with people who are having a poor effect on you, and you don't have to give them a reason why; you're doing this for yourself, not them.

When It's Working for You

When you've realized you are one with your Divinity, that you are an integral part of the whole, it's amazing how the Law of Divine Oneness begins to work for you. Life flows smoothly and you'll want to get to know people on a deeper level. When we share our thoughts and beliefs with one another, we can agree, disagree, or agree to disagree, but still respect one another as unique individuals making our way through life. You'll find that things which were once difficult to obtain seem to flow toward you with ease. There is a sense of peacefulness within your soul. You won't worry as much, will be less critical of others, will tend to avoid drama, and conflicts will seem to happen less often. You trust in your intuition instead of looking to others for answers and believe in yourself instead of seeking the approval of those around you.

We have to remember that we are living in the earthly plane and will make mistakes along the way. It's part of the process of spiritual growth. No one is perfect and we can't expect to be in this realm of existence.

The other part of the process is acknowledging your bad days, owning your actions during those times, and learning from them. Once you understand the concept of the Law of Divine Oneness, it will always be a solid part of your core spiritual essence, along with the feelings of peace and love it brings. Try not to beat yourself up over errors in judgment because that will only dim your own inner light. Work through it, learn from it, and move forward with grace.

Try It Now

Sit with your eyes closed and imagine the grandness of the universe. Think of all the people sharing the earthly plane with you; consider the animals, plants, rocks, and everything that makes up the world. Feel the energy of these things surrounding you. Now imagine your own vibration blending with all the others. Feel this energy move through you, through the world and into the universe. Imagine the entire galaxy vibrating in one ultra high frequency. You are one with all that is. Let this feeling of Oneness brighten and shine within you. Enjoy this feeling for as long as you'd like, then slowly open your eyes, keeping the feeling of Oneness inside you.

Practical Application Tips

- Let your individual light shine through random acts of kindness to teach by example.

- When you are connected to Divine Oneness it can bring an end to hatred, jealousy, and other negative emotions.

- Put aside thoughts that you're better than anyone else. We are all part of the Divine.

- Choose to see past all differences in others and only see them for the spiritual being they are. Do this for an hour at first, then a few hours, then a whole day. Eventually, it will become second nature to you.

- Make an effort today to not speak aloud anything critical, judgmental, or negative.

- Make a list of the things you fear. Work on letting go of those fears by addressing each one individually and finding the reason for the fear.

- Honor someone else with respect for their opinions, even if they differ from your own, through honest consideration even if you ultimately agree to disagree.

- If you've built barriers against others out of fear of being emotionally hurt, used, or taken advantage of, let the walls down for a while so you can work through the emotions and heal these fears.

- Take better care of yourself. If you're overly critical of yourself, think negatively about the things you do, or allow another's actions to affect you negatively, then you can't fully embrace the Divine within you. When you praise yourself, think positively about your actions, and understand that the other person has to accept responsibility for their own actions and they don't affect you, then you are shining brightly with Divine light. Create your own special mantra to remind you that everything you do affects the Oneness of Being. It could be something like *I am one with all that is and all that will be.* Say it every day as a reminder to be the best you can be without harming others in any way.

See Also Chapter 17: The Law of Relativity

3

THE LAW OF GRATITUDE

— ❧ —

Today I express love and gratitude for the
people in my life, the things I've received,
and the joy these blessings have brought me.

THE LAW OF GRATITUDE states that in order to get what you want
in life, you have to be truly thankful for what you already have. When
you show gratitude, you are rewarded by having your needs and desires
filled in abundance. The Law of Gratitude means you must be sincere
in your gratefulness. This gratitude has to come from deep within you,
from the heart of your soul, and it must be felt through every fiber of
your being. Just saying *thanks* without true gratefulness behind it does
not work; you have to mean what you say. Spiritual gratitude is feeling
appreciation for everything—it's thankfulness of being, of consciousness, and of the Divine.

The Law of Gratitude has been prevalent in many religions from their beginnings because they evoked a core human emotion which enabled them to gain followers. To worship with thankfulness from the heart, in gratitude, is a common theme in Christian, Jewish, and Buddhist religions to only name a few. For those who don't follow any set religion but who believe in spirituality concepts, living the Law of Gratitude helps keep them on a Divine path.

The Law of Gratitude enables you to move forward with purpose, a positive attitude, and with joy in your heart. Spiritual gratitude is powerful because it draws abundance and positivity to you. If you practice it every day it becomes an embedded part of your being.

Your thoughts and feelings are made of energy. As you send this energy to the universe, the universe will send you more of the same because you appreciated it when you received it the first time. So if you are truly thankful for the delicious buttered biscuits on your plate, don't be surprised if the waitress brings you more without you asking for them. When you're grateful for what you have, then asking for more is a request that the Divine is willing to fulfill.

Living in Gratitude

Let's take a moment to look at the connection between the Law of Gratitude and the soul's purpose. When you're living in gratitude and are truly grateful for everything in your life, the depth of your emotions is the catalyst that can take you to greater heights of Oneness. Gratitude becomes part of your spiritual essence, it changes your perception and allows you to attract more blessings for which you can be thankful. Gratitude can help you remove negativity because when you give appreciation for that negativity, your light shines on its darkness and sends it scrambling out of your way.

Positive and negative energies are in everything within the universe, both living and inanimate. Being spiritually grateful means you don't deny the negative while unconditionally accepting the positive. You have to know how to react to and counter negativity with your own positive energy when you encounter it. By denying its existence, you're denying yourself the ability to counteract it with love and light. This means you also have to acknowledge your own negative feelings by looking for their source so you can understand where they're coming from and why you feel that way. Only by doing this will you be able to work through the negative emotions and change them to positive ones by understanding them and appreciating the lesson they've taught you.

We experience life with others who are on the same path so it's important to recognize the gratitude and support you're receiving from others. We are interconnected to thousands of people, some of which will come and go while others are with us for extended periods of time. When you're grateful for each of these people and their individual purpose in your life, then you can learn lessons from these relationships. Some lessons will be easy while others will be more difficult. Be thankful for each lesson because it will cause you to grow on a soul level. When you're willing to give of yourself, to feel gratitude for others, you can appreciate them in each moment. Let them know how you feel and how much their support means to you.

Forgiveness Is Gratitude

Forgiveness is a big part of gratitude. When you are able to forgive others for their negative emotions or actions and are grateful for their role in your life (even if the situation was a difficult one), it's easier to release any negative emotions you may be holding onto because of the relationship. Forgiveness opens the door to gratitude and allows you to move to a higher spiritual frequency instead of hanging onto the hurt that keeps you at a lower frequency.

What if you were the one that caused another to feel emotional pain? One of the most difficult tasks on our spiritual paths is to forgive ourselves. You do this by first owning up to your actions. Looking at the situation from a place of gratitude can help you see where you went wrong. Once you've taken responsibility for what you did and see it clearly, then forgive yourself and appreciate the opportunity to right the wrong. Then, if possible, ask forgiveness from the person you hurt and let them know how much you appreciate the role they had in helping you grow spiritually. This can be really difficult to do because sometimes it's simply not possible to reconnect to the person, and if you do, you will have to accept their decision. They may be unwilling to forgive you, but that's their path and lesson. Regardless of the response, you'll feel more at peace because you've forgiven yourself and feel gratitude for the experience.

When you're living the Law of Gratitude it's also important to release any feelings of resentment you have by looking at the situation from a different perspective. Feelings of resentment can block and consume you if you let them. Resentment means you feel ill will towards another person or a situation because you feel wronged, whether that wrong is real or imagined due to unfulfilled expectations or a sense of entitlement. It's hard to be grateful when you're placing blame somewhere else because your own feelings fill you with negativity. Once you release these feelings you'll be open to allow the positive energy of gratitude to surround you.

It's important to also be honest with yourself about gratitude. Are you truly grateful or are you just saying you are? Gratitude gives you the power to create anything you want in life. Gratitude increases your frequency, so when you ask for positive things to come into your life, you're at a vibration where it is easier to recognize and receive them. Without gratitude your inner power is weaker, and you may not see opportunities or spiritual gifts when they appear because you're too wrapped up in negativity. The universe has unlimited abundance and energy to share with you if you're thankful for it.

It's important to realize you deserve what you're trying to accomplish. Try not to settle for less by having an undeserving attitude. You deserve everything you want and then some! If you just sit back and accept life as it happens and believe it is *fate* or *destiny* holding you back, then you're not realizing your full potential. When you're not moving forward to achieve your goals, you're just settling for whatever happens because you're not willing to do the work needed to succeed. This often happens when your feelings of gratitude are low. Boost your gratitude, know you deserve all you can achieve, and you'll reach your goals. Don't settle for less—instead, work hard to make all your dreams a reality.

When you want something in life, you are drawing upon your own energy and asking the universe to supply you with the extra energy you need to accomplish your goals. If you'll only ask for what you want, move forward in strength, positivity, and with appreciation for all, you can achieve and receive everything you want in life.

Try It Now

The easiest way to show daily gratitude is by making a list of the things you enjoy doing, the people you love, and even the things that annoy you. Now take time to go through the list and express your thanks for each item, one at a time. Speak the reasons you're thankful for each listing out loud because the spoken word is powerful. When you can appreciate even the things that annoy you, then you're truly applying the Law of Gratitude and the results can be transformational.

Practical Application Tips

- Make a daily gratitude list. If you have limited time, choose one thing or person in your life that you're grateful for and give it/them your appreciation and thanks all day.

- Set goals for yourself, give thanks for those goals every day, and imagine yourself achieving those goals with gratitude and love.

- Imagine your energy merging with universal energy to create a super high vibration. By working together with the universe, you'll make it easier to obtain your desires.

- Tell yourself that you deserve what you're asking for each and every day.

- Challenge yourself. When you set daily challenges and express appreciation for your ability to step up to those challenges, then you're making yourself happy. Happiness and gratitude go hand-in-hand with successful achievements.

- Stop thinking about what you want to do to accomplish your goals and take action. You can think something to death but you need to take actions based on those mental plans to achieve results.

- Be conscious of what you receive every day because of the gratitude of others. Give your gratitude in return.

- Expect the unexpected. Sometimes the most unexpected things bring tremendous amounts of gratitude and joy.

- To bring more to you, give thanks for what you already have. Constantly asking for more without appreciating what you have can hold you back from acknowledging or receiving more blessings in your life.

- Be present in each moment, stop trying to control every aspect of your life, and be open to receive the great things that can be yours if you'll only ask and then work toward achieving those goals.

See Also Chapter 40: The Law of Potential

4

THE LAW OF LOVE

— ❧ —

Today I am true to my spiritual essence;
I am a beacon of love. It radiates from deep
within me to touch all I encounter.

LOVE IS ONE OF the purest frequencies. According to many different religions, the origin of love goes back to the beginning of time, to the act of creation and the love that the Creator felt for what was created. You cannot see it, touch it, or contain it. You can only experience, observe, and feel its effects. With your heart filled with love you can reach the highest levels of spiritual awareness and growth. It is unconditional, purifying, immense, and all powerful. It has the ability to heal, cleanse, and is the power of creation. Love can bring people together, turn an enemy into a friend, mend relationships, and elevate your Spirit. Love is dynamic. The more you love, the more that love grows in depth and strength. It expands to encompass all that is around you, above and below you. It can grow to unlimited proportions until you feel as if you're a being of love, which you are.

Sometimes on the earthly plane we tend to forget we are love. It's more than just an emotion we feel, more than just romantic love, the love we feel for family and friends, or love for the things we enjoy doing; it's who we are as spiritual beings. It is our nature to love everything we encounter; from other people to plants, animals, our environment, and the things we enjoy doing. The list can go on and on because love is infinite. They say the eyes are the window to the soul so let the love in your soul shine through for all to see. You don't need to say anything because love is radiant and will be acknowledged and understood by other spiritual beings for what it is. Sometimes words can be confusing, they can place restraints on love or cause uncertainty. Instead, send your love infused energy to another to convey your feelings. Sometimes a loving look says it all.

Love improves our lives and gives more meaning to our existence. It is a state of consciousness that, when shared, can elevate those around us to be more in tune with their own spiritual existence and the essence of love within them. As we share our love with others and they share their love, then the world becomes a more peaceful and loving place. Exponential growth is possible through love and the participation of the masses can heal the world.

Don't think that by showing love to others you won't have enough for someone else. When you share love, it grows and enhances your life. The supply of love within you, within the universe, is infinite and inexhaustible. It will never run out. It will only increase the more it is used.

Learning through Love

The Law of Love gives us the opportunity to learn through loving others. When things don't work out in a romantic relationship you may feel brokenhearted but if you love yourself, that self-love will heal you and see you through the situation. Love should never cause you distress. In every relationship there will be times of ups and downs. It's how you handle the situation that's important. If you view the difficult times with love, then the two of you can work together to resolve problems so your relationship will grow stronger. Love should never cause anyone physical or emotional pain, or make someone feel belittled or less than the wonderful Spirit that they are. In these kinds of situations, rely on the love you feel for yourself. Decide if the relationship is based on the real essence of love or if there are conditions. Love is unconditional. Sometimes love means letting go and moving forward to learn the lessons needed to grow spiritually.

Fear of not being loved by others or of being alone can cause people to stay in relationships that aren't balanced, positive, and in forward motion. When you release this fear the power it holds over you disappears and you'll see life clearer and from a loving perspective. What you give freely and unconditionally to others will return to you in abundance. The more you give love, the more love you'll have to share with others. It is your gift to give.

Love is not about what you will receive from another person so you feel valued. You don't need someone else to validate your worth. Love is about the feelings of joy and happiness you can give to another without expecting anything in return. This doesn't mean you must take care of their every need. If you do then they may begin to feel dependent upon you and eventually resent your help because they may feel as if they're not being all they can be as a person. They may want to break free of the relationship to seek out their true self again. Love means giving, supporting, and encouraging someone while letting them be their own person.

Love and Acceptance

The Law of Love means to let your actions speak for you. When you love another person without expecting them to love you back, then your actions are showing the person how much you care and that there are no conditions on how you feel about them because you love them for themselves, not who you want them to be. The Law of Love means total acceptance of another person or situation. This means you are accepting of the person's differences, faults, quirks, likes, and dislikes even if they are totally opposite from your own. When you accept someone through the higher consciousness of love and appreciate them as a spiritual being, you're living the Law of Love. The same thing applies to situations you find yourself involved in; if the situation is one you find challenging or stressful, look at it with love to reduce the stress and help you to see the best steps to take to meet the challenge. The Law of Love can help you in many different ways; all you have to do is approach the people and situations in your life with love instead of fear, defensiveness, hatred, or charged emotions.

Move Ego out of the Way

How are you supposed to practice the Law of Love when there are so many egos you will encounter on a daily basis? Some people may be boastful, proud, troublemakers, instigators, or have other negative aspects to their personality and a sense of self-worth that is in direct conflict with your ideals and your own self-esteem. You start with yourself. Put your own ego aside, feel the love inside you, let it grow and spread throughout you until it is flowing out of every pore in your body. Imagine yourself as a stream of consciousness that is pure love. Allow this essence of yourself to wash over those around you, sharing your love with them. Now look at the people around you, find the loving essence within them and connect to their Divine Spirit instead of the personality they are projecting on the earthly plane. Do not judge them or try to change them, instead send them unconditional love. Oftentimes, this helps ease interactions with difficult individuals. Once you do this, you're living the Law of Love and encouraging your own spiritual growth. Loving yourself does not mean you become so full of self-love that you're gloating about yourself, become a braggart, or think you are the be all and end all of humanity. Don't let your own ego get inflated.

Sometimes letting go of ego is easier said than done. I've been on the spiritual path for many years. I always try to do the right thing and send love and positive energy to others. But I have to tell you, there were many times when I was challenged quite a bit. There have been plenty of times when I have had to bite my tongue when someone was acting negatively toward me. I don't always win this battle and neither will you. It's part of human nature. But as long as you're trying to live the Law of Love and you're succeeding more often than not, you're on the path of spiritual soul growth. Sometimes it'll be two steps forward and one step back. Just keep moving.

Love is all around you, it's an integral part of the universe we live in, let it live in you.

Try It Now

If there are ever times when you feel lost and like you've gotten off track from the Law of Love, take time to re-center yourself. You can do this by visiting an elderly person in a nursing home. The appreciation of having a visitor, someone to talk to, to tell their life stories to, will be reflected in their eyes. Or look into the eyes of a baby, who hasn't experienced any of the negativity of the world yet, you'll see love in their eyes too. Or look into the eyes of an animal. There's love there as well.

Practical Application Tips

- Treat those you love with dignity, respect, and honor. Anything else is less than love.

- Let your love shine through your words and the way you speak them.

- There is no ego in the Law of Love. Share your love without conditions or expectations of what you'll get in return.

- You must truly love yourself before you can share your love with others. Connect with your inner essence to find self love.

- Your actions will always mean more than your words.

- Love is not selfish. The Law of Love means to share love from the heart with good intentions.

- Love does not cause pain, negative feelings, or low self-esteem. If you're on the receiving end of this type of a controlling situation, which is often referred to as love, when it's not true universal Divine love, re-evaluate whether you need to remain in this situation or remove yourself from it.

- The eyes are the window to the soul. Look for the love inside in your interactions with others.

- Love is shared with all that resides in this world so don't forget to give your love to the animals, plants, and everything else in the natural world.

See Also Chapter 1: The Golden Rule

5

THE LAW OF FREQUENCY

— 🕊 —

I choose to embrace my lightness of being,
to bring my frequency to the highest possible
realms of infinite vibration by surrounding
myself with goodness, positivity, and light.

THE LAW OF FREQUENCY means that pure energy is at the foundation of everything in existence and this energy vibrates at a frequency unique unto itself. The faster the energy vibrates, the higher the rate of frequency. One of the maxims of *The Kybalion* states, "Nothing rests; everything moves; everything vibrates." Not only does this apply to the things you can see, touch, and hear but also to your emotions, thoughts, and actions. Your frequency is different from the frequency of a plant, chair, or rock, yet each of those things is made up of energy moving at subatomic levels. Sometimes it's difficult for us to believe in things we can't see unless science finds a way to prove it is true, but even with the unproven, there is power in belief.

Frequencies are harmoniously attracted to one another, and because of this attraction, they can move into higher rates of vibration, or in the case of negative attractions, into lower ones. It is worthwhile to raise your frequency to attract higher frequencies to you. If you are dominated by positivity then you'll receive it back in abundance; if you are dominated by negativity, you'll get that back in abundance as well. Positively altering your thoughts raises your frequency and changes the flow of energy to you, helping you to become more successful. Spiritually, your unique frequency is your energy at a soul level. Your true essence is the basis of your frequency and is exceptionally high as Spirit. Living on the earthly plane affects your frequency; every experience you have had affected your frequency positively, causing it to increase, or negatively, causing it to decrease in vibration.

Frequency Focus

Ultimately, as spiritual beings we are striving to elevate our consciousness and frequency to the same high level it is on the spiritual plane. At times this can be difficult because the earthly realm has its own unique challenges. As you learn more about your own spirituality and focus your attention on raising your frequency you will soon be able to determine your frequency level immediately. You will know if participating in a certain activity will increase or decrease your frequency. If you need assistance with this, please check out my other book *365 Ways to Raise Your Frequency*, which contains daily exercises that will raise your frequency to find more balance, purpose, and joy in your life.

If you think of frequency in terms of positives and negatives, it's easier to understand how each thought, action, or feeling affects your frequency. Emotions like confidence, joy, bliss, happiness, and love are filled with high vibrations of lightness that move quickly, increasing frequency. Fear, jealous, hatred, doubt, and impatience have low, heavy vibrations that move slowly, which decreases frequency. Intentionally increasing high vibrations by choosing to be confident instead of afraid, or to love instead of hate, raises frequency. Your active choice to be positive instead of negative brings more positivity to you, thereby raising your frequency.

How Others Affect Your Frequency

When you surround yourself with others who are upbeat and in forward motion, they are inadvertently helping you to raise your frequency. On the other hand, if you're surrounding yourself with people who surround themselves with negative thoughts and emotions then that rubs off on you and will lower your frequency. Try to never compromise your personal integrity and values because someone else is trying to lead you down a path you really don't want to travel. You'll feel the most comfortable around people who have the same frequency you do. If you want to elevate your frequency, seek out those whose frequency is higher than yours. These may be people who have already attained the success or values you seek, they may be people who are more spiritually open and aware, and who can teach you to tune into your own spirituality. The more you connect with higher frequencies the more you'll raise your own and draw to you the positive successes you're striving to achieve. When you connect with people of higher frequencies it may feel a little strange at first. This is because your frequency hasn't reached the same level yet. As you learn from them and your frequency rises, you'll feel like you're on the same page with them once your frequency adjusts to the higher vibration.

Intuition and Self-Awareness

The Law of Frequency means becoming aware that everything around you affects your frequency. You'll instinctively know when a situation, person, or your own thoughts and emotions are increasing your frequency because you'll feel happier, lighter, stronger, and more powerful. If it's lowering your frequency then you'll feel worried, upset, condescending, or just mad at the world. When you're aware, you'll be able to stop yourself from feeling these types of emotions and mentally make a power shift within yourself to replace a low vibrational emotion, thought, or action with a higher one.

This type of self-awareness at a soul level is an integral part of implementing the Law of Frequency within your spirituality. Another way to be more self-aware is to recognize that everyone has their own path to walk in this lifetime. You can be kind to others even if you choose not to participate in their negative approach to life. Your kindness may be exactly what they need to turn their negative attitude to one of positivity, thereby raising their frequency. Helping others to heal, move forward, and embrace the higher vibrations of life has to start somewhere and with someone. You may be the catalyst to help someone to be all they can be. Let the Law of Frequency empower you on a spiritual level.

Choosing to understand the Law of Frequency and attaining a high level of frequency enables you to make changes you may not have previously considered. You'll feel more in tune with everything around you. To attract what you're striving for, focus on the positive ways you can make them happen. If you want a new job that pays a six-figure salary, take actions that will put in you a position to attain that job. Do you need to learn a new skill for the job or learn to manage money in order to grow the money you have into wealth? By matching your frequency to that of your dream job and working hard to achieve it, makes the process easier. Don't think *I want this* or *that* and it'll be handed to you on a silver platter. Some goals are easy to achieve but others take work.

Belief and Intention Affect Frequency

Belief and intention are important parts of implementing the Law of Frequency. Believing you will receive what you're striving for and that you deserve success, financial freedom, a well paying job, or anything else, followed by a belief in seeing yourself achieve those things assists in bringing them to you. Positive intention is equally important because it helps you adjust to the changes in vibration. If your intentions are self-centered, too competitive, or negative, you'll find that change happens slower or not at all. You may feel like you're struggling. To fix this, examine your intentions and make internal changes to release negative thoughts or the way you approach achievements. As you work with the Law of Frequency you'll be primarily working with your spiritual frequency, your higher self, and beliefs at a soul level. You may become more involved with learning about topics on a deeper, more meaningful level. You'll also discover more about your emotional, mental, and physical frequency. I call these areas the Core Four. Each of them will empower your overall spiritual growth as your frequency rises.

When you understand the Law of Frequency and implement it into your life, anything is possible. You can achieve your goals, dreams, and ambitions if you work within the understanding and flow of like attracts like. Know that your frequency is constantly rising to bring what you want most to you.

Try It Now

Think of a goal you met. As an example let's say that this goal was to get a raise in the amount of money you make at your job. Did you put in more hours than necessary? Did you provide amazing customer service? Remember how your energy felt as you strived to achieve the goal and when you actually received the raise. Did it elevate even higher? Did you feel a sense of joy surrounding the accomplishment? Now choose a new goal you want to achieve. Let the higher frequency of meeting the last goal flow with you as you manifest the next goal. Frequency builds upon itself to make accomplishments easier to reach.

Practical Application Tips

- Make sure your emotional, mental, physical, and spiritual frequency are all in alignment. If one of the Core Four is not at the same vibrational level as the other three, then raise it so you'll feel more centered and attuned to your frequency.

- Be truthful and pure in your intention to achieve fast results.

- Take the time needed to adjust to how the increase in your frequency feels to you.

- It's never too late to live within the Law of Frequency. Start raising your frequency today.

- The vibrational energy you send into the universe will attract the same frequency back to you. Purposefully send out higher vibrations.

- Everything is in motion, nothing is static, change is constant. To become more in tune with your frequency, quiet your mind and feel the flow of energy and its vibration within you.

- Trust in your spiritual self and intuition as you live the Law of Frequency. As Spirit, you know how to get your frequency back to the level of infinity. Trust in yourself to follow that path.

- Let frequency draw you. If you feel a strong desire to do something or to be at a specific place, follow that feeling to find opportunities to raise your frequency.

- Remember as you align yourself with universal frequency, universal frequency is also aligning itself to your frequency. When this alignment happens, anything is possible.

See Also Chapter 12: The Law of Harmony

6

THE LAW OF
INTENTION

— ❧ —

I do not want, I do not wish. Instead, with
the purity of my soul and the power of the universe,
I intend and allow for all that I am and all that
I desire to be made into reality in my life.

THE LAW OF INTENTION states that the entire universe is made up of energy and information. The reasons for what you do and say are the basis for the Law of Intention. The more focused, clear, honorable, and pure your intentions are, the faster you'll receive what you want in life. Thoughts and ideals, purpose and path, are the way to achievement. The Law of Intention clears your pathway to allow smoother and faster progress. In yoga this law is also called the Law of Intention and Desire, and yogis are able to control specific functions of their body through the use of this law. They may increase or decrease their blood pressure, heart rate, or breaths per minute. You too can practice using the Law of Intention by purposefully intending to slow your rate of breathing.

Wanting a goal and intending to attain that goal are two different things. Let's say your goal is to clean your house. If you want to clean your house, or wish your house was clean, it will be easy to put it off or let someone talk you into doing something else instead of cleaning. Thinking of cleaning your home with a wishful intention is unfocused, weak, easy to put off, and can make it take a very long time to complete the goal. Wishing doesn't have a lot of motivation or purpose behind it to attain a desired outcome. But if you *intend* to clean your house, you have the power of the universe backing you, and nothing will stop you from getting your house clean in record time.

The Power of Intention

Intention has extreme power. It fills you with a strong sense of purpose and an urgency to take action. Intention will enable you to reach your goals quickly if properly used. The best way to make your intention work for you is to focus your energy, feel your core spiritual self, and decide with positivity that you will make what you desire happen. Feel the frequency of this decision radiate through you and then move away from you as your frequency seeks out the frequency of your goal. It's not enough to just think you want something. You must *intend* to achieve it and that intention should be specific, clear, and focused. When you work from within your own spiritual energy source, this is working with intention.

Be attentive to your intentions. It's easy to get distracted but if you put your attention on something it will grow stronger, if you take your attention away from it, then it flounders. When you stay focused on your intention, making sure it is pure and not misguided, you're giving your energy the ability to transform into something more powerful. It's important to be honest with yourself about your intention. Are you doing something just to be recognized for it? Do you have a secret hidden agenda for your actions? Are you giving people you don't really like preferential treatment because you think they can help you achieve your goals? It's harder to achieve goals if you've got ulterior motives behind your actions.

Often you'll receive what you want when you can prove that you'll be able to handle what you're asking for. If you're trying to increase your salary at your job, but you squander away the money you already make and end up short each month for the bills, then you're not showing responsibility with your salary. But if you get your spending in check, come up with ways to earn extra cash on the side, and have a surplus of money at the end of the month, then its apparent to universal energy that you can handle more money so more will come your way. Remember the universe will not just hand you what you want. You must earn it by showing you can handle it.

Intention also applies to how you treat others. When you give someone your word, make a promise, or you tell someone you'll be somewhere at a certain time, then do your very best to follow through. You are putting your intention of keeping the promise or showing up out into the universe as a commitment of intention. Living the Law of Intention means you are living with your focus and attention in the present with positive purpose of being. You're projecting positivity with pure intent into the future in order to achieve the things you want for yourself in this lifetime. This means living in the moment while projecting your intention for future achievements. It's also a good idea not to get attached to the results you'll achieve because you may receive more (or less) than you requested.

Types of Intention

In medicine, the word intention refers to how a wound heals. There are three kinds of medical intentions: a primary intention is when the edges of a wound heals without granulation because it has sutures, a secondary intention is when the edges are separated and granulation occurs to fill in the gap between the edges and epithelium tissues grows over the granulation, thereby creating a scar, and a tertiary intention is when granulation tissue fills in the space between the edges of the wound but the epithelium tissue grows over the granulation slower, usually because there was a delay in obtaining sutures or because the wound is infected, thereby producing a larger scar than you'd have with a secondary intention.

Now let's take this information and apply it to the Law of Intention. If you are living in a primary intention, you are aware of what is happening in your life, you take quick action to fix things that need fixing, you intentionally project good, positive thoughts, and take action because you feel it's the right thing to do, not for what you think you can get in return. Because of this, you obtain your desires. If you are living in a secondary intention, then you don't take action as quickly as necessary because you feel that things will work out if you give it a little time. You allow negative thoughts to lead you at times instead of looking at the positive. You tend to see the truth of situations pretty quickly and while you may have a little scar from an experience you tend to see the lesson in it and move forward with positivity. If you're living in a tertiary intention, you're in denial. You take the wait-and-see approach too far and often stay in situations that are not beneficial to you out of a sense of obligation or because you don't want to face the truth of the situation. Your sense of purpose may be floundering because you're doing things because you want something in return. Your motivation may be negative. Because of this, like a wound that festers, you may feel like your life is festering around you, that nothing good ever happens to you or that you deserve the bad things happening to you. If you're in a tertiary intention, now is the time to clean out the wound, soak it in antibiotic solution, and start the healing process. You may have a big scar, but that scar is a sign of the struggles you went through to heal. Change your intention and your motivation to change your life.

Try It Now

What I'd like for you to do is to write down five situations you're involved in. It could be something as simple as stopping by the grocery store to pick up something for dinner or as complex as a relationship. For this example, we're going to the grocery store. Think of your intention as you head to the store. You have to get milk and eggs. As you walk in, there's an elderly person behind you. Do you continue into the store or stop and hold open the door? At the milk aisle a lady is trying to decide on which milk she wants. Do you cut in front of her and grab the milk you want or do you wait until she's finished and then select your milk? If you chose holding the door for the elderly person and waiting for the woman to select her milk, then you're living from a place of pure intention. Now look at your list of five situations. Write down your intentions, your motivation, and sense of purpose about each one. Be completely honest. This is an exercise to look deep into your soul at who you are and how you choose to live.

Practical Application Tips

- Do not demand that the universe fulfill what you intend to receive. Ask and then let it go, allowing it to happen.

- Keep your ego out of your intentions. When ego is involved you'll think about what you can get out of the situation instead of what you can give.

- Who you are at a soul level, your spiritual essence, will attract energy of the same frequency to you. To change and improve upon what comes to you, enhance your spiritual being.

- The more virtuous, forgiving, loving, reverent, sincere, kind, supportive, and aware of universal truth you are, the deeper and more pure your intention.

- Being greedy and wanting more and more will block you from receiving. Give and be happy with what you have and suddenly you'll find that more comes to you when you're least expecting it.

- Just be yourself, live in your truth and embrace your spiritual essence. God and the universe will do the rest.

- In order to achieve all you want, you have to let go and allow what you've requested the time to grow in form and come back to you.

- Attachment and expectation can block results. Use intention instead.

- Be of service, expect nothing in return, and your blessings can be enormous.

- Never think that someone owes you because you helped them. Help them out of unconditional love, which is the purest intention.

See Also Chapter 28: The Law of Attention

7

THE LAW OF ATTRACTION

— 🕊 —

I feel the frequency of my desires as an
integral part of my soul energy. As my
frequency resonates with the energy of what
I need in life, the desires I'm manifesting
come to me and become part of my reality.

THE LAW OF ATTRACTION is probably the most well known of the universal laws of nature. It has been in existence since early Greek and Roman times. At that time, it was kept hidden from the general public in order to control them and keep them from realizing that they controlled their own destinies. The Law of Attraction states that what you put out into the universe will come back to you. It means you will attract people, situations, and things that are at your same frequency (energy vibration) through belief, creative visualization, and passionate attention. The Law of Attraction embraces the concept that like attracts like and you will attract things with the same frequency as your spiritual self. So if you're filled with positivity you will attract positive energy but if you're filled with negativity you will attract negative energy.

It's important for you to look at your core beliefs, your habits, thoughts, relationships, actions, and intentions to see how you are being affected by the Law of Attraction. Do you often see the silver lining of possibilities even if things aren't going as you'd like? Do you take a negative attitude that everyone is out to get you? How do you handle compliments? Do you accept them happily with a *Thanks so much!* or do you brush them aside because you feel uncomfortable or undeserving of the praise? If you discover your habits tend to lean negative more than positive, it's important to become consciously aware of your thoughts and actions and turn them positive by looking at the opposite of the negative habit. For example, if you're always late, make more specific plans so you will arrive earlier. Making little changes will help you have more positive, enlightening, and fulfilling experiences instead of negative ones.

The Power of Thoughts and Words

The Law of Attraction means you can manifest anything you want by giving it a purpose in your life. By making it part of your essence it can't help but be drawn to you. You have to go deeper than just wishing for it or wanting it but by using the Law of Intention with the Law of Attraction, you can intend for it to become part of your life.

I've always believed that thoughts and words have great power and once said, cannot be taken back. You've sent them on their way to do their job of bringing whatever you said back to you. I try not to say things that are hurtful, condescending, or negative. I also try not to say worst case scenarios or think about them because by doing so I'm giving that negative possibility the power to manifest in my life. I much prefer to look at the best possible outcome and talk about it as if it's already happening. By doing this, I'm using positive intention and manifestation to bring that situation into my life.

Retelling Experiences

While we're talking about thoughts, let's discuss retelling things that have already happened to you (I've had people ask me about this a lot). The Law of Attraction says that what you say will come back to you. Will you draw that same energy to you again by retelling the event? What if that situation is negative and not positive?

In my opinion, there's nothing wrong with telling someone what happened to you as long as you're just saying the facts and not wallowing in despair about a negative situation and expecting the other person to feel the same anger or frustration you may be feeling or making them feel bad about themselves because you're boasting about your success. As a friend, they are there to listen, offer words of encouragement, or propose other points of view or possibilities that could lead to your own enlightenment regarding the situation, *not* to feel what you're feeling. If you expect that kind of reaction from them, you're embracing negativity instead of overriding it with the positives you learned from the experience. In return, be the same sounding board for them when they need to talk. As you discuss events, you can come up with a plan of action that uses the Law of Attraction to counteract the bad experience so that it turns into a positive learning experience. Always end these types of conversations on a positive note.

Another saying is *be careful what you wish for*. This concept is very important in the Law of Attraction. How you phrase something can make a huge difference. It is more effective to say *I have more money* even if you haven't received any extra yet, than to say *I wish I had more money*. Thinking and speaking as if you have already achieved the results you want is the quickest way to make it happen.

Waiting ... Universal Time
Is Different from Earth Time

With the Law of Attraction you also have to remember that the universe's time frame and your time frame are not the same. Universal time moves at a much slower rate. You may want something today but the universe thinks you should get it in a year. You can't be attached to the outcome, the length of time it takes to manifest, or be impatient, when working with the Law of Attraction. You must be active in striving for your dream. You have to give up control of the outcome the moment you begin manifesting it, but you still need to work toward achieving what you're manifesting. Some people believe all you should do is put the thought out into the universe, give it power by believing you have achieved the results, and then just wait for it to show up. If you're not passionate about what you want to manifest, it could take forever and a day to get to you. When you are passionate, constantly putting your energy into achieving what you want on a daily basis, and doing the work required to help it along, it will manifest in your life at the perfect time, which may not be the time frame you had in mind at the time you originally manifested it. There are also times when you may be manifesting one thing but the universe follows your life map that you planned prior to birth and gives you what you need, not what you want.

There are plenty of skeptics of the Law of Attraction but that's because people try to use the law without really understanding how to use it. Living the Law of Attraction is deeper than just being a positive thinker who sets a goal and waits for it to arrive. You have to want your desire above all else and creatively visualize yourself being or using what you're manifesting. Some believe that once you visualize what you want to manifest, you can let it go and occasionally put yourself within the emotion you feel when you think about achieving your goals. Others believe you have to wake up every day with your mind on what you're trying to achieve and then passionately take steps each day to attain what you want. Both are active ways that will work. When you're an active participant and raise your frequency to match your goal, it's easier to attain success.

Try It Now

I believe you can manifest at any time and in any place. You don't have to set aside quiet time in order to manifest. So, wherever you are right now, as you're reading this, stop, think about what you want to manifest, your positive intentions for wanting to receive it, and the gratitude you'll feel when you receive it. Ask this thought to go out and find what you're asking for and bring it back into your life when the time is right. Imagine your manifestation thought leaving you and going out into the universe to do as you requested. Now that your manifestation is complete, you can finish eating your lunch, knowing that what you want will come to you when the time is right.

Practical Application Tips

- Own what you want to attract with your words. Saying *I have* or *I am* is much more powerful than saying *I wish* or *I want to be*.

- Don't say it if you don't mean it. Conviction is a powerful tool. If you're not 100 percent convinced that you'll receive what you're asking for, then don't ask for it.

- Passion equates to possibilities. If you're passionate about what you want to draw to you, then you're doing your part in the Law of Attraction.

- Manifesting requires that you feel, believe, and live your desires. It's not enough to half-heartedly ask and sit back to wait. Nothing worth having is delivered without some work on your part.

- Creative visualization, especially when it's done with intense positive feelings of passion, is one of the best ways to manifest your desires.

- Surround yourself with like minded people who believe in the power of positive thinking, manifestation, and working hard to attain what you want in life.

- If you run into skeptical people, you can choose to keep your thoughts about the Law of Attraction and manifesting your desires to yourself. Don't allow their negative energy to derail you.

- If people think you're dreaming too big, don't listen. Go big or go home. Live your passion.

- Give equal amounts of time thinking about what you want to manifest and your feelings about manifesting that item.

- Understanding and patience is required with the Law of Attraction. You may feel that things aren't happening even though you've been trying and trying. Give it time. And if you receive a replacement for what you asked for, appreciate what you received. For example, let's say you wanted a new car and had a Jaguar in mind but you received a Fiat. It doesn't matter what kind of new car you received, it's still a new car, just not the model you wanted. Find your gratefulness for what you received.

See Also Chapter 37: The Law of Cause and Effect

8

THE LAW OF
ABUNDANCE

— 🕊 —

Today I connect to the abundant Source of
all that is. I willingly remove all blocks and
am open to receive all the happiness, love,
and joy of the universe with positivity. I am
one with the abundance coming into my life.

THE LAW OF ABUNDANCE states the universe is just that: infinitely abundant; everything and anything you can imagine is contained in the universe in unlimited amounts. This flow of abundance continually moves toward you; all you have to do is receive it. The universal stream of consciousness, of knowledge, ideas, emotions, and things we can manifest into our lives never runs dry, even with millions and millions of people dipping into the stream. If you can imagine it, the Law of Abundance can provide it. In ancient history, the Chinese would enact the Law of Abundance by doing an exercise where they'd write down the things they wished to obtain in the coming year. This practice has become what is now referred to as the Chinese Law of Abundance Check.

When you put yourself in harmony with the Law of Abundance by resonating at the same frequency you are able to reap its benefits. Sometimes this means letting go of old notions and releasing ideals to embrace new ones. Anything that is happening internally will manifest externally so your emotional state should be healthy and in forward motion for the Law of Abundance to work and help you recognize the abundance you've already received.

Avoid Blocking or Underestimating Yourself

Take a minute to consider this statement: *You are the only one standing between yourself and everything you've ever wanted to obtain or achieve in your life.*

You are so much more than you may realize. Never underestimate yourself or the power of your spiritual essence, mind, and conviction. All of this is combined into one physical body, which can sometimes feel very limiting. This limitation serves a purpose. It pushes your spiritual boundaries, forcing you to see and feel what lies beyond the physical. Your thoughts, attitudes, and way of being when it comes to how you think about abundance in your life can either set you free to achieve unbelievable heights or can stop you right in your tracks.

If you feel as if you don't have enough time, money, friends, happiness, or anything else, then you've set yourself up to have a *lack* mentality which essentially keeps those things from coming to you. If you have an *abundance* mentality then you will get everything you need plus everything you desire because you believe you will. Sometimes a lack mentality is conditioned in us. You may feel it is selfish to take care of your own needs before taking care of the needs of others; therefore, you've had a lack mentality programmed into you in this life or a past one. When you become aware of these pre-conditioned feelings within yourself, and realize you don't have to keep thinking this way, then you open yourself to receive abundance. If you have a strong work ethic and believe anything is possible, you will feel encouraged by the abundance all around you.

Let's say you are standing at a fork in the road and the sign on the right says, → *Abundance and Prosperity This Way*, and the one on the left says, ← *Lack Mentality This Way*. Which path do you believe would require the most energy to take? The answer is neither. It would take the exact same amount of energy to step to the right as it would to step to the left. So if it's not going to require any additional energy, why would you choose a lack mentality over abundance and prosperity? Well, it could be you have a mental or spiritual block, which makes you choose left instead of right. If you feel you don't deserve to have abundance in your life then you'll always walk away from it and simply accept thinking with a lack mentality as your fate.

You Control Your Fate

Remember this: Your fate is in your own hands. It always has been. You mapped out your lifetime prior to birth and there is a lesson to be learned if you're choosing lack over abundance, but you have to figure it out so you can change your path. Don't let the terms, fate, destiny, or luck be an excuse for not facing the truth within your soul lesson. You deserve all the universe offers. Believe it in your heart and soul and don't let anyone tell you otherwise. Keep your head up and don't listen to the naysayers. They are your temptation to fail. Be strong and carry on.

The Law of Abundance is not only about money or material things. It's also about receiving an abundance of love, joy, gratitude, and knowledge. It means becoming completely and infinitely aware of the energy within you, of your true spiritual essence, and following the path that you've chosen for this lifetime. It's about accepting, receiving, and feeling blessed by the gifts given to you. It's about having an abundance mentality instead of a lack mentality. It's about allowing good things into your life while eliminating the things preventing you from receiving abundance from the universe. This is why many old souls no longer focus entirely on material wealth. It's a *been there, done that* situation. Younger souls still have to go through the desire for the material in order to experience the same lessons and spiritual growth that older souls have already experienced.

If you think in terms of lack or that you're undeserving of abundance then you may decide you're being punished by God and the universe based on some negative behavior in this or a past lifetime. While it is true that you may have additional lessons to learn based on past lives, the universe doesn't penalize you. Instead it responds to the energy you send out.

Ways to Practice Receiving Abundance

Practice inviting abundance into your life. Use the term *I invite* at the beginning of each sentence when you're requesting what you want. When you issue a warm, welcoming invitation, you're clearing the pathway for abundance to flow into every part of your life instead of just waiting around on the perimeter for you to receive it. I've always believed the quickest way to obtain what you want is to ask for it. Whenever I went on job interviews I always made sure that I asked for the job and I always got the jobs I really wanted. When you ask for what you want, it's easier for it to come to you and for the universe (or employer) to provide it. If you don't ask, then your intention isn't clear, when you do your intention is crystal clear.

When you are ready to accept abundance you will receive it. If not, then you'll need to do more work to remove any blocks or to prove you can be responsible with the abundance you want to receive. The universe wants to make sure you can responsibly handle the gifts it is going to give you. So take time to think about whether or not you are ready for the things you're asking for or if you need to do more internal work first. Once you've invited abundance in are you keeping it from actually reaching you because you're not receptive to it? Are you acting according to negative expectations of what you anticipate happening instead of allowing abundance to do its job? If you are, this can affect the abundance you receive. If your expectations are positive then you're not preventing abundance from reaching you. If you want to attain success then attune to the frequency of abundance.

When you think of the Law of Abundance remember it is your connection to the Divine and the frequency radiated there. It is being able to openly receive love, joy, happiness, and positivity at a core level, which will radiate to all areas of your life. The material things will come once you're connected in Spirit to the infinite abundance of the universe.

Try It Now

This exercise is to remove limitations by consciously releasing them in order to freely accept abundance. Think back to your childhood. Write down everything that felt limiting or fearful to you. What were you taught about money, relationships, people who were richer than your family, success, your work ethic, morals, right and wrong? Include any ideas that you weren't taught in this lifetime but feel ingrained in you. Spend some time on this list, maybe even a few days, really thinking about your core beliefs. Once your list is finished, go back to it and ask if the idea is true, a fear, or limiting. Do most other people agree with what you've written down or is it something only you believe? If you feel what you've written no longer applies to you, or was something you believed because someone else told you to believe it, then let it go. Consciously release it and replace it with a new thought that welcomes abundance. As you do this exercise you're actually healing your perception and outlook so that you're ready for the abundance you deserve.

Practical Application Tips

- Focus your attention on the abundance you want in your life with a positive, deserving attitude.

- Align your energy with the frequency of universal abundance.

- Let go of any lack mentality thoughts.

- Practice inviting abundance into your life.

- Heal yourself to allow more abundance to come to you.

- Open your awareness of your fears; remove fear to bring peace and abundance.

- Sometimes you can try too hard to force abundance to come to you, which has the opposite effect. Try but not so hard that you block yourself.

- The more you hold on to any resistance you're feeling about accepting the Law of Abundance, the more resistance you will find. Let go of each resistance as you become aware of it.

- Focus on emotional, mental, and spiritual abundance first in order to make abundance of the material easier later on.

- What you are inside is what you will manifest and receive on the outside. Be one with Source inside for abundance to flow outside.

See Also Chapter 19: The Law of Compensation

9
THE LAW OF LIGHT

I am Divine light and love. As my light
shines into the world, it clears the way
for me to help others as we all strive to reach
our utmost achievements in this lifetime.

THE LAW OF LIGHT means that by transforming your consciousness and connecting to your own inner light, the light of the universe, and the light in one another, you'll open yourself to empowerment, knowledge, and a deeper connection to your own awakened consciousness. Throughout time it has always been believed that light will defeat darkness. This concept that goodness will always triumph over evil has been an integral part of both wars and religion. The Law of Light means understanding and expressing yourself in a spiritual way through the Divine light of the universe. It means embracing your Divine radiance within and expressing it without.

Light reveals truth, uncovers that which isn't easily seen, it guides the way in the darkest of times. It is an indication of higher consciousness, individual spiritual growth, and the illumination, understanding, and connection to your higher self. The Law of Light urges us to become one with our own inner light, through the process of accepting who we are, where we've been in this lifetime and past lifetimes, and acknowledging what we've learned in regards to our life lessons. As you embrace your inner light, you in turn will become a beacon to others. They will be drawn to your light and from you they will learn to embrace the light within themselves.

Higher consciousness develops in a methodical way. The more you learn, the more aware you are of your own inner light, the more you're connected to the light of advanced perception. Once you've passed from the lower levels of self-consciousness into a state of awakened, higher consciousness, you are empowered by universal light. This empowerment is fundamental in your own awakening. Light is at the core of existence. People who have had near death experiences talk about walking into the light. It opens your awareness to concepts you may never have considered before now, raises your frequency, strengthens you, and can lift you to higher levels of enlightenment. Universal light is Divine.

Light for Protection

The Law of Light is strong and pure. Using the light from Source, God, and the universe, you can shield yourself from negativity. Using light for protection can help keep negative energies or emotions at bay. Its purity blocks impure energy. Most people use white light but you may find yourself drawn to other colors such as gold, blue, or purple. You can use light to protect your spiritual essence at any time. You don't have to do a complex meditation ritual or set aside a specific time to protect your energy with light unless you want to. I generally have limited time available so when I use light as protection from negativity, it's done in a matter of seconds, at any time during the day or night. I see it as a lightning bolt or beam of light entering through the top of my head, filling and surrounding me in an instant.

Creative visualization is how you'll harness the power of light to keep negative energy at bay. In your mind's eye imagine light flowing to you from the universal Source. Allow it to quickly flow over your head and seal itself underneath your feet. As it's creating a bubble around you, give the light the intention to protect, strengthen, and serve your energy as needed to keep you safe from negative emotions, influences, or another's energy. Then release the light to do its job. You can boost your energy shield as needed. You can expand your bubble of protection to include your vehicle and other people if you feel the need to do so.

Many people with empathic abilities use light to help keep the emotions of others at bay. This is because other's emotions can be an energy drain to an empath. If you are an empath, as you develop and learn to control your empathic abilities you can also use light to help calm an emotionally distraught person or to help balance their energy by adding your light to their own to strengthen them. Since this use of light is more involved than protection from negativity, it is a good idea to always ask their permission before using light in this manner.

Lightness of Being

There is something I call *Lightness of Being* which is both part of your spiritual growth and a catalyst in drawing your desires to you. Spiritual light isn't something you can see with your physical eyes but instead see with your mind's eye. It is something you feel intuitively. When you're connected with universal light, your whole being feels lighter, happier, buoyant, and at peace within yourself. This Lightness of Being carries over into every part of your life. Troubles are less troubling, problems are less problematic, solutions are found easily, and goals reached with ease. When you are filled with Lightness of Being, you become a magnet for high levels of positivity, which brings with it abundance in the form of your goals and desires which can manifest into your life. Lightness of Being means you're no longer burdened by heavy emotions, negativity, restrictive thinking, or blocks along your path. When you're filled with Lightness of Being you will laugh more often, experience less setbacks, see the world as a grand place filled with possibilities, you don't dwell on the negatives in life and are more resilient. You no longer expect the worse. Instead you always expect the best possible outcome in every situation. When you do experience difficulties, they are resolved quickly and efficiently.

Light and Love

From a spiritual perspective, light is as unconditional as love. When we talk about unconditional love it means you feel the essence of love in everything you do without holding on to any preconceived notions of what it is or isn't. You do not hold anyone to certain conditions or specifications when it comes to unconditional love. You either accept them as they are or you don't. If you don't, you leave them behind and they are no longer part of your life. It is the same with universal light. There are no conditions on spiritual light. It is there for you to connect to in order to come to a greater understanding of your own spirituality, to use without limitation for protection, and it can illuminate your pathway while on the earthly plane of existence so you can learn your life lessons, accomplish your dreams, and live a life filled with Lightness of Being.

Once you have unified your inner self to the light and love of the universe, it becomes an ingrained part of your inner essence that you're not consciously thinking about. It is as much of a part of you as taking your next breath, which you're often not aware of either. It becomes second nature in its existence within you, involuntary, and automatic.

As you become more enlightened and understand the importance of being of higher consciousness, make sure you're staying grounded in the physical world even while opening to the wonders of universal light. It's easy to get caught up in healing and working with light to help others and the planet while forgetting to take care of yourself. Maintain a clear focus and live in a practical state of realistic enlightenment. Accept the power within you, know you can be successful and feel at home with both your spirituality and your physical existence.

Try It Now

To open your senses to the universal light within you, close your eyes and feel the warmth and brightness of your inner light at the heart level. Imagine yourself looking at your energy, see how it vibrates around you. Now look deeper into your energy until you reach the level of your soul essence and feel the connection between it and your mind. Can you see your soul's inner light in your mind's eye. What colors do you see? Is it clear, white, or does it have colors within it? Allow your light to radiate from your center into every part of your spiritual essence, let it warm and invigorate you. Now feel your inner light move from your spiritual core essence through your frequency, the vibrations of your energy, until you feel it radiating within your physical being. Feel it flowing into your arms, legs, from the top of your head to the tips of your toes. Feel its high frequency and the quick vibrations as it moves through you. It gives you a sense of purpose, of being. You are at one with your spiritual self and the universe. Now open your eyes. See the light in everything around you. Let this feeling stay with you always.

Practical Application Tips

- Find your inner light, understand your uniqueness, your frequency, and let your light shine into the darkest corners of your life, filling every part of your being with hope, love, and joy.

- Connecting to universal light is quick, easy, and can be done at any time. Don't make it harder than it is.

- Release fear, anxiety, and misgivings by filling these emotions with universal light.

- Light can heal anything if you'll only let it.

- Choose a mantra that helps connect you to the light of your soul essence.

- Try seeing universal light with your eyes closed. Now try seeing it with your eyes opened. Once you can easily see it in your mind's eye with your physical eyes opened, you can tap into its positivity at will.

- To see the light in another, look in to their eyes. See them for the spiritual being they are inside.

- Use universal light to increase feelings of joy, happiness, and your sense of wonder.

- The purest request for assistance happens when you request help from universal light. Be pure in what you ask for and thankful for the results.

- Do not put conditions on universal light. Accept it as it is, love it as it is, and become one with it as it is. Trying to change it into what you want it to be instead of what it is, will block your progress.

See Also Chapter 25: The Law of Responsibility

10
THE LAW OF UNITY

—— ✦ ——

*Today I will look for the Divine light in everyone
I encounter. I will see the brilliance of their inner
essence and let my own light shine for all to see.*

THE LAW OF UNITY states that we are all part of one spiritual being with each part working together for the whole even though the parts are different and unique individually. Spiritually, we are the same and are connected to one another because each of us has the same Divine energy within us. The Law of Unity recognizes our spiritual essence, the form we inhabit in the spiritual realm. The Holy Bible, King James Version, speaks of the Law of Unity in Genesis 11:5–6 when people worked together to build a city. Other religions also believe that when people come together to attain a common goal, that the goal will be reached.

When we exist in the physical, on the earthly plane, we are so far removed from our higher self, our spiritual awareness and knowledge of the Divine that it is easy for ego to focus on the differences between us, thereby creating division, instead of unity. It's hard enough for us to recognize, accept, and embrace our own spirituality and Divinity, and it's even more difficult to see it in others. This is one of the challenges of living in the physical realm and is why the Law of Unity is so important to understand and live by. As you begin to recognize the Divine light in others, the Law of Unity helps you to feel our interconnectedness which results in helping others. Being connected by the Divine gives a greater understanding of oneness, the unified connection of every living person on the planet, and the knowledge that each of us is on the same path back home.

Unity Reflects Oneness

The Law of Unity means to look at the oneness of the parts of the whole instead of seeing each as a separate entity. If you look at life this way, every person on Earth is a sibling, a child of God, the Source, or universal energy. As we look at the whole, we also no longer see things in extreme differences but instead see and understand the *process* of the difference. For example, if you look at your idea of right and wrong and then compare it to someone else's idea of right and wrong you may discover they are completely different based upon where the other person grew up, their morals, ideals, and other extenuating influences upon them. Does it mean you're right and they're wrong or vice versa? Or can it be you're both right or maybe you're both wrong? When you start to question ideals based on a universal point of view, you start to see the process of how people believe and think the way they do. The differences between us are acknowledged by the Law of Unity while stressing the importance of recognizing we are all part of the whole, of the Divine.

Conquering Fear through Unity

Fear of things that are different or that we don't understand is the primary reason there is a separation between spiritual beings on the earthly plane. To eliminate the fear, we must make an effort to understand these differences. With understanding comes the removal of fear. When you look at the people in the world through fearful eyes, you may feel you are all alone in the world, that no one understands you and you must keep yourself closed off from other people. If this is the path you're on, now is the time to take a new direction. When you close yourself off from others, from understanding the Divinity within them and learning from them, then you're also closing yourself off from experiencing your connection to the Source of creation. Eliminating fear encourages soul growth and a reconnection to your essential spiritual self, including your connection to the Divine.

Whereas fear can block you from experiencing the Law of Unity, love can encourage you to embrace it. At its basis the Law of Unity means you must feel love in your heart for all that is. Love brings understanding, forgiveness, and the ability to see through barriers placed before you. If you love someone you help them when they're struggling or even when they're doing great just because you want to be there for them and enjoy them in your life. Love combined with the Law of Unity expands your ability to express love, caring, and understanding further into the world. It will surpass your circle of family and friends to reach people whom you've just met or who you will never meet but who will be positively affected by your actions.

Put Ego Away to Live in Unity

What does your mind think of the concepts of the Law of Unity? It pretty much reels back in disbelief that you'd ever consider such a thing and may even feel threatened by the concept. Ego will probably fight you in the beginning, but, once your ego sees deeper than the physical and emotional differences between people, and concepts such as love, hate, right and wrong, then living within the Law of Unity becomes a part of your being and the ego no longer feels afraid or threatened so it shuts up in acceptance. Ego is the face you put on for the world to see, not who you are as a spiritual being.

When you live with your ego in the forefront you may find you're always looking for approval from others or you may feel you have to control every aspect of the things you do or the people around you. Ego gets upset when you experience criticism, even constructive criticism, because ego takes that personally. When you live your life with the Law of Unity in the forefront, you see criticism as something to work with to improve upon yourself or the task you're doing. You don't take things personally, don't need someone else's approval to add to your own self-worth, or feel like everything has to be your way or the highway. Instead, you consider all angles. You understand that what someone else says may be helpful instead of hurtful because everyone is the same inside and is part of the whole. Ego feeds on perceived power; your Divine light is true power. Life is easier when you follow the Law of Unity. You are more in tune with your own Divine light and are able to see the Divinity in others. This means you'll experience less conflict because you no longer fear the differences between you. You feel safe and secure in your own Divine nature. Living the Law of Unity has it challenges but when you are secure in your own inner self, your own Divinity, and you see everyone as the same and part of the whole, then your reactions change for the good of all. You will make different choices, your reactions will become more positive in nature instead of reacting in like kind to negativity, and you'll find you're filled with more joy and happiness. Living the Law of Unity is like pouring gasoline on your Divine light and striking a match, firing it up with positivity. When you live from the core part of your spiritual self, it is easier to get what you want in life. It simply flows to you and you readily accept it, just as you accept everyone else as part of the whole universal energy.

Try It Now

To practice the Law of Unity, try this exercise to see the inner light in others. Go to any public place like the mall or a park where there are a lot of people moving around. Find a bench or chair where you can take in your surroundings, see how people are interacting with one another or how they behave if they're alone. As you observe other people, feel the energy they're emitting. Are they quiet, loud, laughing or arguing? Once you sense their mood, try to feel their energy and look deeper for their inner light. Is it shining brightly and uninhibited or is it dimmed by emotion? After you've observed others for a while, take a moment to imagine your own Divine energy growing and radiating from you. Imagine it moving forward into the crowd, showering everyone it meets with love and positivity. Now notice if anyone looks over at you. If they do, offer them a smile and say hi. Notice what kind of response you receive in return. They may smile and say hi back or they may feel awkward and look away when you look back at them. That's okay. You know that your light has touched them and hopefully has added a little brightness to their day.

Practical Application Tips

- Hold the door open for someone.

- Engage in a conversation with a complete stranger. Let your inner happiness shine through. The conversation may be very short but if they smile you've accomplished your task.

- Choose one thing you're afraid of and make a concentrated effort to eliminate that fear.

- If you encounter someone who is angry, annoying you, or are causing problems in your environment, focus on sending your Divine light towards them in a calm manner. Your energy will affect them and they'll either move away from you or you'll notice a change in their behavior. You don't have to say anything.

- Become aware of your ego. Feel the difference in how your ego presents yourself to others and how you are when you're alone and being your true self. Try to live each day as your true self even when interacting with others.

- Try to work through emotions such as jealousy, envy, and bitterness in your life. When they come up, focus on why they have presented themselves and listen to what they are trying to get you to notice. Without working through these emotions, they block your sense of Unity with others.

- Look past the differences in others to see the person inside.

- Be more understanding, patient, and respectful of others to see their Divine light.

- Try not to judge others but instead think of how you'd feel in their shoes.

See Also Chapter 29: The Law of Forgiveness

11

THE LAW OF PURPOSE

—🕊—

I look inside my sacred self, my core soul
essence, to discover the purpose given upon
my soul's creation. I will live my life to realize
my purpose which brings me joy and fulfillment.

THE LAW OF PURPOSE states that everything in existence was created with a purpose and has the ability to fulfill that purpose. This law is also known as the Law of Dharma that originated in Vedic Hinduism mythology. The purpose was ingrained within the core energy contained within everything and everyone during creation. For us, this means that when our spiritual being was created from Divine universal energy, our purpose was programmed into that energy. This happened long before your spiritual being ever considered physical incarnations so it is part of your core spiritual essence.

I believe the Law of Purpose is multi-layered and that you can have both a primary purpose and many secondary purposes. In life, you wear many different hats and have many different passions which all contribute to your overall individuality. These are your secondary purposes that help you connect to your primary purpose, which is being true to who you are at a soul level.

It's a common belief that what you do in life is your purpose. The way you're perceived by others, the toys you're able to gather, and the success you achieve in your job. While all of these are results achieved by fulfilling secondary purposes, they're not what ultimately defines your principal purpose. Each of us has distinctive qualities, gifts, and aptitudes that helps us express our soul purpose in unique and creative ways. In expressing our purpose and living our lives with purpose, we draw the things we desire in life to us.

Living with Purpose or Spiritual Purpose?

Is living life with purpose equivalent to our spiritual purpose? They are different because one is external and the other internal. When you live your life with purpose you are confident that the things you want in life will become yours. This confidence, along with your aspiration to reach goals, is what will propel you to achieve what you want. It is your inner drive and desire. Your spiritual purpose is the reason for your existence. What is the most basic, primary purpose for your existence on the physical plane? It is to reconnect with and awaken to the genuineness of your spiritual being, listen to the guidance that comes from your core energy within, and to realize you are a Divine being while experiencing life in a physical form in a physical world.

Being focused on external things like making money, garnering attention for yourself, or the things you accumulate in your life can keep you from recognizing your true purpose, which is internal. Look past the external to see into your soul. Be courageous and confident as you pursue your spiritual purpose because sometimes your purpose may not be something that is globally accepted. Part of my spiritual purpose is to teach others about their psychic abilities, the paranormal, and spirituality. These themes are not globally accepted as scientific fact even though they exist. My path hasn't been easy, but it has always been fulfilling to know that I've helped someone in some small way by shedding light on experiences they've had but didn't know how to define.

How Others Help Your Purpose

You'll encounter many people in life who will either knowingly or unknowingly help you fulfill your primary purpose. These people may be teachers, employers, friends, neighbors, even strangers you encounter in your daily activities. You may not even realize it but you may also be helping them fulfill their purpose while they're helping you to fulfill yours. This also goes back to the Law of Divine Oneness in that we're all part of the whole and the whole works together. It's important to live in the moment of each day so that when these helpers, teachers, and guides appear, you recognize them for who and what they are.

When you give up your happiness in order to do what someone expects of you, then you are no longer fulfilling your soul's purpose. When this happens you may feel unfulfilled, like something is missing inside. Day after day you go through the motions; you may feel overwhelmed, easily frustrated, and anxious. By reconnecting with your soul essence and primary purpose, your happiness will return. You'll wake up each day excited about the strides you'll make and the delight you'll feel in what you're doing. There is a sense of satisfaction associated with following your spiritual purpose.

I'll use myself as an example to illustrate. My soul purpose is to teach. I feel fulfilled when I'm helping others by teaching them something they didn't know or clarifying something they didn't understand. This is especially true in regard to metaphysical topics because I didn't have anyone to guide me as I struggled to learn about and understand my own abilities. I teach others about spirituality and how to understand their intuition through my books. When I'm able to assist others on their own unique paths, then I am achieving accomplishments related to my sub-purposes which bring me happiness and fulfillment. This is in line with my soul purpose of awakening to the truth of my inner spiritual being.

Discovering Your Purpose

If you're not sure of your purpose, how can you discover what it is? Think about who you are and what you do. What word defines who you are at a soul level? Once you choose this word, then everything else is what you do in life. If you're not sure, you can begin by making a list of the things in your life that make you happy or that you're passionate about. You will see a theme emerge within the entries. Also make a list of the rules you set for yourself. Make two headers, one for things you always do and one for things you'd never do. As you compare these lists what theme do you see? Take your time and your purpose will become apparent. You'll probably realize that you've known what it is all along.

Sometimes you might get stuck when trying to figure out what you're supposed to do in this lifetime so here's a list of some of the most common themes relating to finding your purpose to help guide you: artist, athlete, caregiver, creator, horticulturist, humanitarian, intellectual, leader, musician, scientist, teacher, warrior, working with animals.

When you are living your purpose you'll feel as if you're helping the world and humanity in some way, you'll feel like you're making a difference in the lives of others and in your own life. Compassion, paying attention to how you interact with others, and living at a high vibration will ensure you're living your purpose. Sometimes you may feel that you're making great strides and other times you'll feel as if you're taking small steps. As long as you're always moving forward, you're on the right path.

You might realize your purpose when you're feeling conflicted emotions or are involved in negative circumstances. When you feel torn or see the meaningless in negativity it can elevate you to a higher frequency where you're able to see past these things to the core of your being and the real reason you exist. That is when you can take action to make changes that will further enable you to realize your soul purpose. It's easy to lose the connection to your spiritual self while on the earthly plane, especially if you are caught up in negativity and are out of balance. Living your purpose feels like you're completely in harmony with yourself, the world around you, other people, and the universe as a whole. Living your purpose with passion opens the door to endless possibilities. You can achieve all your desires when you're living your purpose and living your life with purpose.

Try It Now

Find a place where you can sit uninterrupted when no one else is around. Think about your life. Go back to a time when you felt you were on the right path, when you were filled with your own inner power and you were making a difference either in your own life or the lives of others. It is a time when you felt a calm peace within yourself. You were happy and fulfilled. When you think of this time, think about what you were doing that made you feel these things. If there were other people around you, what were they doing? Were their actions helping you to fulfill your purpose or were you acting on your own and helping them? When you examine a time in your past where you were happy and fulfilled, you'll find keys to unlocking your life purpose.

Practical Application Tips

- Make a list of the things you're passionate about to help determine your purpose.

- Think back to when you were young. What excited you? Did you love writing, drawing, or sports? Things from your past that you no longer do can help you discover your purpose.

- What are some of the things you enjoy today that you can get so engrossed in doing that the time flies by? These activities can be a key to your purpose.

- Reconnect to your spiritual self through meditation or quiet time.

- Take time to tune into your innermost thoughts and desires, things you've never shared with anyone.

- Consider if you're not pursuing your purpose because you're afraid of what someone else will think or say about it. Worrying about other's people's opinion when it comes to living your purpose can hold you back.

- Take action to fulfill your purpose. You can't live your purpose if you're not acting on it.

- Know what is important to you. What are your values? Your moral code? If you're not sure, write it down to gain insight into your purpose.

- Experience the unknown. When you take the time to experience new things it can help you find your purpose.

- Realize that your primary purpose, getting in touch with your spiritual core being, never changes, but your sub-purposes, the things that bring you joy and you're passionate about, and help you achieve your primary purpose, often change over time.

See Also Chapter 27: The Law of Faith

12

THE LAW OF HARMONY

— ✦ —

*Every experience gives me the opportunity to grow
spiritually. It is my choice to restore stability if I'm
out of balance and to create harmony in my life
which allows me to achieve all I need and desire.*

THE LAW OF HARMONY relates to balance through energy. Everything within the universe is balanced. The Law of Harmony means the balance between opposing forces, which according to the *Kybalion*, is the same way harmony is found in the Law of Compensation and the Law of Cause and Effect. These forces can be external to you and within your environment or they can be internal emotions, ideals, and thoughts that affect your actions. The Law of Harmony means that as an energy being you are able to align yourself with universal energy, which opens you to receive supreme abundance. Anything and everything is possible and attainable when you've achieved core alignment through the Law of Harmony.

When something is out of balance in the universe events happen to restore the balance and bring harmony back to the situation. Nature is a perfect example. A smooth lake is in balance but if a storm crosses the lake, the wind causes waves and the rain causes millions of tiny splashes which create additional ripples across the surface of the lake, temporarily making it out of balance. As the lake absorbs the new water and the wind dissipates as the storm passes by, harmony is restored to the lake. Because of the storm, it has gained something new, the additional water, and is forever changed by experiencing the storm, but it returns to a balanced, harmonious state.

You can apply this to your life as well. When you experience a situation that temporarily alters your life, as you align yourself with the event you may be forever changed by the experience but you can bring yourself back into balance and restore harmony. Every experience is an opportunity to learn, grow, and reflect. If you're not living in harmony you may experience fear, problems in your communications with others, or you may feel conflicted, mistrustful, lonely, sad, or alienated.

Letting Go to Feel Harmony

One of the key elements in living the Law of Harmony is to let go of fear and negativity. If you're afraid of something it will be difficult to feel the harmony of the universe because it is often the basis of other negative emotions like jealousy, envy, and worry. You can choose not to allow anyone to cause you fear or to control you through fear. You always have the ultimate choice of achieving harmony in your life and if it means letting things go, then let them go. Let's think about negative emotions for a minute and how you can work through them. What if you're jealous of someone? Think about why you're jealous. Is it because you feel they may try to take someone you love away from you? Or is it because they have things you want but are afraid you'll never be able to attain? If you think about your negative feelings you can always determine what's causing them if you dig deep enough within yourself. Once you know the reason behind negative emotions, you have the opportunity to release them and replace them with something positive. Sometimes that means deciding you will not let another person's actions make you feel any less about yourself. If the person you love doesn't love you enough to remain faithful to you, then maybe they're not the right person to have in your life. If you're jealous of the things another has because you're afraid you'll never be able to achieve the same things for yourself then decide you can either live without them or strive to attain them. Then, instead of feeling jealousy toward the person, feel happy for them that they've been able to achieve those things for themselves and let their success inspire you. When you have happiness and joy for another's accomplishments then you open the door to achieve your own goals, and attain happiness and joy for yourself. You restore harmony into your own life and reap its rewards.

This is how you can tell you're living the Law of Harmony and are in sync with the harmonious nature of the universe. You're now intentionally seeking harmonious energy. If you're not adding to the harmony of the universe then you're taking away from it through negative actions and emotions. Another way to think about it is that everything you give to others you are creating for yourself. However, it's important to realize that if you're giving negativity to others, you're also creating negative situations for yourself. Remain on the side of positivity to achieve everything you want.

Harmony Is Based on Love and Action

The Law of Harmony is also based on love. When you send love out to everyone and everything around you, then you'll receive love in return.

Love is such a positive emotion that it can lift you from despair into joy. Start by really feeling love for yourself and for the world around you. Then start sending unconditional love to others, from your heart to theirs, and then release it. The energy you send to them will positively affect them and it's a great way to elevate your own frequency. Another important part of living the Law of Harmony is that your emotions and thoughts must be realized through your actions. Think of your thoughts as physical things that result in action and directly affect you and those around you. To be successful in your achievements, your thoughts, emotions, and actions should all be aligned together. Are your actions reflecting something different than what you thought or felt? If they are, it's time to dig a little deeper into your true spiritual essence. If you're truly in harmony you aren't going to want to treat another person in an unkind manner. If you're out of balance, your soul searching will help you figure out the problem within yourself and rectify it.

The Law of Harmony means you make conscious choices that will not limit you in any way. If you're placing limitations on yourself then you're blocking your own success because you're making it harder for what you're trying to achieve to get to you. It's like building a wall around yourself. To open the flow of energy so it's easier for you to reach for your goals and for your goals to come to you, try some of the following choices when the opportunity arises:

- Choose to treat everything and everyone in the universe with honor and respect. By doing this, you're honoring and respecting yourself as well.

- Choose to accept that things will happen in life. When they do, don't let them affect you in a negative way, instead look for the positive.

- Choose to be adaptable. When you are, then you can easily flow with the movement of life instead of against it.

- Choose to show tolerance, friendliness, and kindness to your fellow man.

- Choose to live life without limits.

- Choose love.

- Choose to see the value in all things.

- Choose focused calmness over drama.

Once you've been working on living in alignment with the Law of Harmony you'll begin to notice that life is flowing smoothly, everything just seems to happen easily and without much drama. Help comes along just when you need it the most in the form of important information or a helping hand of a friend, acquaintance, or stranger.

Try It Now

Think about an area of your life that feels out of balance. First think about a reason why this area is out of balance. Once you have the reason, decide on an action to take that will help bring this area of your life back into balance. Once you have the solution keep considering the area that is out of balance. Is there anything else you can do to bring it back into balance? If the answer is yes, think about it again. Repeat this until you feel you have exhausted all avenues to bring harmony to the area of your life that's out of balance. I suggest doing one area of your life at a time so that you can write everything down afterwards without forgetting anything, but if you feel drawn to do more than one area, go for it. At the end of the exercise you will have a plethora of ideas that will help you regain a sense of harmony in your life. Move forward with a sense of purpose and harmony surrounding you. Write down your discoveries and take action to bring them to fruition.

Practical Application Tips

- Take note when you're allowing fear to disrupt your harmony.

- Dig down deep to find the source of your fear. Really analyze yourself and then change the fear into a positive emotion to bring yourself into harmony.

- Send out positive energy and love to others, even strangers, to maintain balance and harmony within your own life.

- As you strive for your goals, don't become so obsessed with them that you neglect other areas of your life. It's easier to achieve goals when you give all parts of your life your attention so you remain in a harmonious state.

- Hold yourself accountable for every aspect of your life. Make alterations as necessary to bring more harmony into your life.

- Act with unselfish intention.

- See and accept every part of yourself as a Divine being. You must find harmony with yourself before you can achieve universal harmony.

- Pay attention to yourself so that when you begin to get out of balance you can quickly bring yourself back to center and regain your balance, which results in harmony.

- Question what you believe so you can get to your own soul truth. When you do, you will find your harmony.

- Accept others as they are. Do not expect or try to make people change.

- When you remove your expectations for what you think they should do, then you allow yourself to be in harmony with their

Divine essence because you're no longer trying to force your will upon them.

See Also Chapter 5: The Law of Frequency

13

THE LAW OF ACTION

— 🕊 —

*Today I will actively take steps toward
achieving my goals. The more action
I take, the closer I am to success.*

THE LAW OF ACTION, simply put, means you must *do* something in order to *achieve* something. In physics, Sir Isaac Newton's Third Law of Motion states that "for every action there is an equal and opposite reaction." To get a reaction, for something to happen, the action has to happen first. You must act to fulfill your dreams, hopes, and desires, and obtain what you want out of life. If you sit back and do nothing, you're not being an active participant which makes achieving what you want difficult. When you purposefully take action, you're aiding the universe by letting it know what you want. It might take a little time but you have to *do* to receive.

It is imperative to understand that someone isn't going to walk up to you one day and say "Didn't you want this? Here you go." That's not how life works even though some may feel entitled to be treated in this manner. When you feel you deserve to have everything handed to you without doing anything to achieve it on your own, then you're not reaching your true potential. There is satisfaction in working to attain the things you desire the most. When you receive them, you know it's because you've worked hard and created what you wanted for yourself. No one else did it, you did, and you deserve to reap the rewards of your efforts.

When you set out to reach a goal, your thoughts and emotions must be aligned with your actions and you must work in an ordered manner toward the goal. If you're not taking action then you need to stop and figure out why. What's holding you back? Are you afraid to start because you think you might fail? Are you procrastinating because you feel the work will take too much effort? You must discover the reasons preventing you from taking action and address why you're feeling this way so you can work through it. Otherwise, it's going to always stay slightly out of your reach. Why? Because *you* have to take action to get what *you* want. No one can do it for you. You may not always take the right action, which is a learning experience, but any action is a step toward attaining everything you want in life. So what are you waiting for? There's no better time than the present to get started.

Start with a To-Do List

Once you start living the Law of Action it will quickly become part of your daily routine. Create a *to-do* list and check it each morning. As you strike each item from the list as completed, not only do you feel a sense of satisfaction for accomplishing something you needed to do, but you're also setting the energy of the universe into motion to bring more things to you because there is now room in your life for them. When you have lots of things to do that you're putting off or not completing, then there's no room in your life for other things to appear. Clear out the old to let in the new.

Your to-do list shouldn't consist only of things you have to do because they're a required part of living like taking out the trash or doing the laundry. It should also contain actions and tasks you can complete to reach your goals. That might include making phone calls, visiting a business associate, or doing something for your neighbor. Even if you don't achieve your final result with one phone call, you're taking action that will bring the final result to you. Even if you stumble or experience setbacks, just keep at it and don't give up. Every little action is keeping you in forward motion. It may not happen overnight but it will happen if you keep at it.

If you're not sure how to get started, the first place to begin is with your thoughts. What do you really want to achieve in your life? If you don't know what you want to achieve then you can't take action. This can result in aimless wandering if you don't have goals to achieve and a purpose to fulfill. You've made a first step by picking up this book. You want to know steps you can take to achieve the things you want in life, but first you have to know what you want. Do you want to take a vacation to the Caribbean? Or would you like to make a six-figure income? Maybe you just want to have less drama and more joy in your life. Maybe you want to obtain all of these! Whatever you want, you can achieve, if you work hard to get there.

So the next question is, what are the right steps? It depends. If you want to take a vacation to the Caribbean then you have to have enough money to pay for the trip so you may have to start saving up for it. Then you'll have to book a flight, reserve a hotel, pack your bags, go to the airport and then be able to relax while you're there so you enjoy yourself instead of worrying about what's going on back home. If you want to make six figures, you'll have to choose a career that pays six figures. You may have to go to school to study for this career, which may give you little time for a social life. If you want less drama and more joy in your life, you will have to eliminate the cause of the drama, be it a job that you're unhappy in, friends who keep you on edge, less social media, or anything else that causes you stress. Let these things go and you'll find that once the drama is gone you'll feel more joy and happiness. Take a look at your own specific circumstances and decide the first step you'll take toward what you want in life. Only you know what you want and the actions you need to take.

Creative Visualization Aids Action

When you think about living the Law of Action and creating what you want in life, you will also think about creative visualization and positive thoughts. They all go together and are part of the process of manifesting. You can think yourself into a stupor if that's all you're doing. I'm a firm believer in creative visualization. When you hold the thought of something and visualize it in your life, you are making it easier for that thing to appear. But if you're only visualizing and then just sitting back and waiting for it to show up then you may be sitting there for a very long time. I believe in using creative visualization combined with action to achieve your goals.

Let me give you an example. We breed Barock Pinto horses. The goal is to have a homozygous tobiano (pinto), and a homozygous black colt because as an adult that colt can be a breeding stallion that will always produce a black and white tobiano foal. Now I could sit back and visualize this colt forever, but I'm not going to get him unless I breed my horses and have foals every year. I also have to plan the breedings by considering genetics to have the most opportunity to achieve the results I want. And even then, the universe can have a little fun with you. Our mares had three homozygous tobiano colts in a row over the past two years, and all were chestnut instead of black. The chance of getting this combination was only six percent. I could have considered that a setback but I don't.

We've already achieved the most difficult DNA combination possible, so the colt we want is bound to happen. The point is that you don't give up on your dreams, you keep going and keep trying. While you may not be able to predict or have any control whatsoever over the outcome, you just keep trying until you succeed. Take action, be proactive in your planning and in the steps you're taking, and eventually you will achieve everything you want in your life.

Believe that you can achieve it, take action to make it happen, and you will achieve your heart's desires.

Try It Now

Choose one item on your to-do list that you have been putting off. Ideally, pick the one thing you dread having to do more than any other. For this example we'll say that you are going to clean out and reorganize a closet in your home. You're dreading this because you know it will take a long time to complete and you'll make a huge mess during the process. Once you get rid of the clutter and disarray contained inside, you free up the energy in your home to flow through that area with ease. Approach the task in an organized way to make the work go faster. Once completed, you'll feel a sense of accomplishment because you took action to reach your goal.

Practical Application Tips

- Stop procrastinating and do something! Even baby steps will help you achieve your goals.

- If you're not sure where to start make a detailed list of the steps you need to take to accomplish a task. Seeing it in black and white helps you to stay on task.

- The action you take depends on what you want to achieve. Stay focused.

- Taking the first step is often the hardest. Once you get started, the rest flows.

- If you get sidetracked, get back on task. Don't berate yourself or start procrastinating, just get back at it.

- Until you take action your success will only live in your mind. You have to act to achieve it in the physical world.

- Give your actions purpose to obtain the most success.

- Add action to your creative visualization to achieve dramatic results.

- Everything has energy and is in motion. You must also intentionally move in the direction of your desires to achieve them.

See Also Chapter 23: The Law of Passivity

14

THE LAW OF AFFIRMATION

— 🕊 —

Today I am motivated and excited to achieve my goals.

THE LAW OF AFFIRMATION states that when you create a positive phrase about what you want to achieve, and you repeat the affirmation to yourself on a regular basis, then in time it will become truth. The Law of Affirmation evolved from the use of Buddhist and Sanskrit mantras in ancient history and today scientific studies back up their usefulness and ability to bring about change. Affirmations can be thoughts or spoken out loud; however, it must be done frequently to live the Law of Affirmation. If you think or say an affirmation several times during a day then it will have a positive and powerful effect on you. It will become part of your essential truth. But if you're only saying the affirmation once a week, it's not going to have the same effect. It will be weaker and take longer to achieve.

You're probably already living the Law of Affirmation without even realizing you're doing it. If you're always telling yourself to *look on the bright side* or *find the silver lining*, these are affirmations to see the good in a negative situation. You've probably said these things to yourself so many times that it's just second nature. The Law of Affirmation works by allowing you to internalize what you want through the affirmation.

The purpose behind the Law of Affirmation is *whatever you think, will be achieved*. It is intended to help you think positive thoughts about yourself so you can feel optimistic and achieve your goals even when you're not feeling very confident. For instance, if your affirmation for the day is *I am happy* yet you woke up feeling a bit blue, by repeating *I am happy* during the day, you'll begin noticing things that make you happy and the doldrums will disappear.

You can use affirmations for inspiration, to change your mood, bring what you want into your life, or inspire you. If you are working on your spirituality then your affirmation could be *I am stronger in my spirituality every day*. Saying the affirmation in this manner lets you connect to universal energy in a positive way and in turn, you will experience more strength in your spiritual growth.

How to Use Affirmations

There are some important points to remember when you're living the Law of Affirmation. It is easy to fall into the trap of negatively affirming things in your life, which is something to avoid if at all possible. When you negatively affirm something, you're bringing that negative thing to you when the goal is to bring positivity to you. Do you recognize yourself when you read these next words? I can't ... I would but ... I don't have ... I'm not ... You don't understand ... I'll try but I can't make any promises ... and so on. Statements that begin like this often end up being negative, and by saying them you're confirming in your mind that they are true. Instead say I can ... I will ... I have ... I am .... Be careful when phrasing your affirmations so they are always positive and without negative words or intentions.

When speaking or thinking affirmations it's important to understand the role of the subconscious mind. It doesn't like change. It would prefer that things continue on as they have been because self-scrutiny is hard, change is uncomfortable, and it's just easier if things stay the same. So if your subconscious mind is more comfortable thinking about all of the things you're lacking when your conscious mind starts thinking about affirmations for the things you'll achieve, your subconscious mind has a little temper tantrum (out of fear) and puts on the brakes. The problem with this is that the subconscious mind is very powerful and can mess up your best efforts by pulling you back into a lack mentality.

Affirmation Resistance

How do you get around the subconscious mind's ability to resist your affirmation efforts? You have to start a little at a time. We recently had a little filly born on our farm. It was the mother's first foal and she had no idea what to do with it and was scared that something or someone was going to hurt the filly. In turn, the filly was scared of us because mom kept putting herself in between us and the filly. She would peek around her mom's back legs to see what we were doing but she wouldn't approach us or let us touch her for very long before she'd run away. This is sort of the reaction you'll get from your subconscious mind if you overload it with too much positivity at once. It will resist your efforts to change. I resolved the issue with the filly by the time she was two weeks old. When a normal approach didn't work, I would talk to her mom but not look at her. When her curiosity got the best of her, she would take a few steps toward me. With my back to her I would reach backwards, palm up. After doing this many times, one day I felt her little muzzle touch my fingers. Each time I'd turn a little until I was finally facing her.

I'd pet her a little further along her body until she realized that I wasn't going to hurt her and that petting was enjoyable for her. If you take things slowly with your subconscious mind just like you would with a skittish filly, you'll discover less resistance to the changes your affirmations will make in your life. One of the ways you can help your subconscious mind adjust is to say things like *I believe, I know, I accept*, and *I realize*. These phrases indicate acceptance of change and will be helpful when you're facing resistance from your subconscious mind.

Just as your subconscious mind can resist your attempts to change through affirmations, you'll also find that people in your life can be resistant to your attempts to create positive change or achieving successful goals. Why? *Because it makes them uncomfortable.* It's not that they don't want to see you doing well and achieving all you want to achieve in life, it's because change can be frightening to some people, causing them to feel bad about themselves because you're doing so well. It all goes back to inner fear. Keep this in mind. You may have to help someone close to you get over their fear of your success.

Make It Short, Keep Quiet, and Believe

When you're creating your affirmations you want to make them short, sweet, and to the point. Long drawn out affirmations are hard to remember and lack the power of a shorter one. Power words are important to use in your affirmations. Your subconscious mind loves and is less resistant to short, powerful, and emotional thoughts. When I use affirmations that are filled with emotion, contain exciting adjectives and adverbs, are short and specific to what I want to achieve, they seem to work faster and with more intensity than affirmations and are calmer, longer, and more generic.

Did you know there is power in silence? When it comes to your affirmations, you don't need to tell everyone what you're doing or what your affirmations are. You give your affirmations more power when you keep them to yourself. You also eliminate having to deal with resistance from those around you.

Belief is the critical component of the Law of Affirmation. Without belief, affirmations will not work. You can affirm something to yourself all day long but unless you believe the affirmation, you're not aligning your energy with the affirmation's energy. Not believing in the affirmation will actually have the opposite effect and can push what you're trying to achieve away from you. Think of your affirmation as the bait and your belief as the rod and reel that will bring what you're trying to hook to you. You must believe that the rod is strong enough to pull in your desires. If you don't, you can cast that line all day but you'll never catch anything. Make sure your belief is true and strong to make your affirmations work quickly and with ease.

The Law of Affirmation means you can use affirmations in any area of your life. You can use them for self-help, situational help, confidence building, and success. Write your personal affirmations with care, take it slow to avoid resistance from your subconscious, and you will achieve all you desire.

Try It Now

It's always handy to have several affirmations to choose from that you can say every day. I have included affirmations at the beginning of every chapter for you to use. Some are a little longer on purpose so feel free to edit them down to fit your needs. What I'd like you to do for this exercise is to create a personalized affirmation notebook that relates directly to your life. Use your own intentions, goals, hopes, and dreams when you create each entry. Buy one of those small notebooks that can easily be carried around with you and then write one affirmation on a page. Open it at random whenever you need an affirmation. Affirmations really can make a difference in your life.

Practical Application Tips

- Make sure your affirmations are in the present tense.

- Affirmations must be personal and apply to your life.

- The intention of an affirmation must always be positive.

- Avoid all negative words.

- Don't use words that imply lack, being without, or any other negativity.

- Be specific in your wording. If the affirmation is too broad it isn't as effective.

- Simple is better. If the affirmation is too difficult to say, it will be harder to put into practice.

- Affirmations should not be impossible to achieve. There should be some slim chance of reaching the goal. For instance, you're not going to grow an extra limb just because you think it would be cool to have one. You can say affirmations for that limb forever but it will never grow out of your body.

- Create affirmations that bring you joy, happiness, and excitement.

- Don't give up. Affirmations take time.

See Also Chapter 30: The Law of Request

15

THE LAW OF CLARITY

— 🕊 —

*With focus and intention I can gain clarity in my life in
order to achieve my goals with purpose and joy.*

THE LAW OF CLARITY states that if you are clear about what you want
to achieve in life, have clear intentions and clarity of purpose, you will
attain your desires, but if you're unclear and without direction or purpose, then it will be difficult to reach your goals. Many religions including Taoism and Buddhism teach the importance of clarity in their
doctrines. Today, you'll find businessmen, professionals, and everyday
people who teach others how important it is to be clear in thought and
purpose to attain your goals. Sometimes you may not know exactly how
to define what you want but you know how you feel about something.
In this case it's important to have clarity of feeling. When you're connecting with the Law of Clarity it's important to speak out loud or write

down what you're trying to achieve or what you feel in a clear, concise manner. Put the thought, words, or feelings into the universe with clear intention. If you don't know what you want and aren't able to voice your intentions to attain it, it's more difficult for it to come to you. The clearer you can be about what you truly want, the more successful you'll be in reaching your goals.

One of my goals has always been to help others gain clarity in their life through intuitive readings or teaching them about metaphysical topics. I've even made the slogan on my website: *Gain Clarity in Your Life*. It's always been important to me to know what I want to achieve and then take steps to attain it. Helping others gain clarity in their life is part of my soul purpose. When you're able to follow the Law of Clarity you'll often discover you'll become more closely linked to your own soul purpose.

The Meaning of Clarity

What does it mean to gain clarity? It means you are focused and know exactly what you want, and it is reflected in your intentions, beliefs, and feelings. When you're clear internally, it's easier to be clear externally through your decisions, actions, and achievements. It means leaving behind confused thinking, uncertainty, or haphazard actions. You are being honest with yourself because you've connected with your soul essence and your inner purpose. Without a doubt you know who you are, where you're going, and what you want to achieve in life. You're pure in your intention, genuine in your action, and live life with a high level of integrity.

Once you're living the Law of Clarity doors open to unexpected opportunities. You understand that if a door closes, a window will open to a new opportunity. You're no longer stuck in unhealthy patterns that hold you back from reaching your fullest potential. You'll also realize people are drawn to you and will tend to want to confide in you in the most unexpected places because you radiate a sense of trustworthiness.

You may be waiting in line at the grocery store when a random person starts talking to you about something that is bothering them. When you're clear within yourself, your intuition will guide you to give them the most helpful response at that moment in time.

When you lack clarity, making decisions can be difficult and you might feel as if your forward motion is blocked. Little things can seem like big problems, you may be forgetful, frustrated, aggravated, easily agitated, overly emotional, or feel as if everything you try to do goes wrong. Lethargy, procrastination, and feelings of being overwhelmed become the norm. If you're feeling like this, now is the time to seek clarity in your life. It will get you back on track, energize you, and enable you to attain your desires.

Steps to Clarity

But how do you gain clarity when it's lacking? Just sitting around waiting for something positive to happen doesn't work. Instead, focus on a goal, make decisions about how you can attain it, and take action. Think about your goal in a clear, precise way and give it your undivided attention, focus, and concentration.

Sometimes you need to take smaller steps. If you are unclear on the direction to take regarding an issue, then clear away any negativity or uncertainty within yourself first. This means to become focused in your thought processes. If you're confused, it's because you haven't really decided what you want or what is right for you in the situation. It's difficult to take action when you aren't sure which way to go. So how do you clear away confusion in order to make the decision? Make a pro/con list. When you write things down you really have to focus on them in order to put them in the appropriate category, which means you have to think and make decisions about what you're writing. When you write it down you're making the thought tangible. You can now hold it in your hand, look at it, and read it until you decide if it's right for you. As you make little decisions, the energy clears for you to make bigger ones.

Worry is one of the biggest blocks to gaining clarity. When you worry about something you're running every possibility that *might* occur through your mind. And it goes on and on and on. Worry keeps you in a state of confusion, of unlimited *what if* scenarios that are without direction or purpose. When you release worry and think with clarity, then it's easier to choose one desirable outcome and plan how to reach that outcome. If you feel like you're doing all you can do but you're still not able to feel clear in your goals, then you may need to simplify the end goal into the individual steps you need to take to reach the final goal. In other words, have a list of little goals you can achieve in order to attain the main goal at the end. If you want to be a lawyer you can't just graduate from high school and then start practicing law. You have to graduate high school, graduate from college, apply and get accepted into law school, graduate from law school, and pass the bar exams. So to become a lawyer there are a minimum of five goals that you need to meet before you can attain your long term goal. When you simplify the long term goal into sub-goals it makes each step easier to achieve.

There are lots of activities you can do to gain clarity. You may enjoy making lists like I do or you may choose journaling, creating a vision board, drawing, painting, meditation, or prayer. Any activity that helps you become focused and clear in what you want in any given situation is what you should do. I know when I'm confused about the direction I need to take I often head out to the barn. There's something about grooming a horse or mucking out a stall that allows my mind to settle, then focus until I find resolutions to issues or determine the path I should take. Often repetitive actions like these (or cleaning your house, washing your car, etc.) allow the mind to come up with creative ways to move forward.

Once you've decided on a goal, give yourself a deadline to reach it and then do something every single day to bring you closer to attaining the goal. If you don't give yourself a deadline, then it's easy to put it off as something you'll do tomorrow or next week. But if you've written it down as a goal to reach by a certain date, then you'll strive harder to achieve it faster. Just make sure your timeline is accurate so you don't end up frustrated, annoyed, and overwhelmed because you put too much pressure on yourself unnecessarily. It's important to pay attention to the path you're walking to achieve your end results and don't forget to stop and smell the coffee or roses along the way. Those pit stops will help you gain even more clarity in your life.

Try It Now

Let's do a creative visualization exercise to help you gain clarity when deciding between two choices. Think of something you need to make a decision about but you're going back and forth on. For the purpose of this example let's say the decision is whether or not you should buy a new car. Close your eyes. Imagine the car you have now and a new car both parked side by side in your mind's eye. Look away from the cars and feel your energy begin to swirl within you. See it as a light mist with white flecks of surging power within it. As it moves around you, let it remove any obstacles that are causing unclear thinking. As you prepare to look where the cars are parked, there will only be one car there. This is the car you need. Now look at the cars. Whatever car you see is the answer to your question. You now have a clear decision and objective in mind and can take action to do what is necessary to attain it.

Practical Application Tips

- Take time to connect to the energy of your core spiritual self to be clear about who you are and what you'd like to achieve in life.

- Write down the goals you have set for yourself.

- The more you think about your goals and focus on the steps needed to achieve them the more power you give them to come to fruition.

- Be specific and detailed in your goal setting.

- Prioritize your list of goals.

- Give each goal a due date.

- Eliminate worry and unorganized thinking.

- Do something every day to create momentum in achieving your goal.

- Stay focused on your goals by reviewing them daily. This gives them power to manifest in your life.

- Disengage yourself from situations and people who aren't clear in their own paths, whose goals are in direct conflict with what you're trying to achieve, be responsible in your own actions and take responsibility for becoming clear and focused and achieving what you want in life.

See Also Chapter 36: The Law of Awakening

16

THE LAW OF SUCCESS

— 🕊 —

*I achieve success through hard
work, with positivity and joy.*

THE LAW OF SUCCESS means you can reach any and all of your desired goals whether they are material, emotional, or spiritual. In 1925 a book titled *The Law of Success* by Napoleon Hill was released in a very limited print run. The ideas in this book were based on other natural laws and led to people using these ideas to become successful. The term Law of Success stuck. To live the Law of Success you have to decide what success means to you in order to achieve it. This is an important question you must answer truthfully, specifically, and with clarity. Some define success as a well paying job, an expensive house and car, and the finer things in life. Others feel they don't need material possessions to be successful. You need to define success for yourself based on your own thoughts, emotions, and goals. The definition of success will be different for everyone and will be right for each individual.

If in your search for success you find you're constantly struggling, then it's time to re-evaluate. Our purpose in this life is to reconnect to our core spiritual being, our Divine nature, and to learn lessons that will advance our soul growth. This is meant to happen without a lot of stress or turmoil. If you feel like life is a constant struggle then you're not in harmony with your true spiritual self, are trying too hard, holding on too tightly in an effort to control the situation, or trying to force your will instead of letting things happen. You will gain the most success if you pursue your objective without trying to control every aspect of obtaining it. There are times when things must happen that are out of your control.

Let's look at success from a spiritual viewpoint first. When you're successful in your achievements, when your frequency is connected and aligned with what you're trying to achieve, then the combined vibration goes even higher and creates a pull within the universe so the thing you want most will reach you. From a spirituality point of view, success means the amount of joy, fulfillment, and spiritual growth you feel when you attain what you want spiritually. This can be spiritual growth, love, happiness, peacefulness, gratitude, joy, finding your purpose, or helping enlighten others. Spiritual success is all about inner growth and positive actions.

Material success is being able to attain the physical things you want in life. Maybe it's a new car, a high paying job, multiple degrees, a boat, house, or any other thing you can work hard to achieve or simply buy if you have earned enough money to afford it.

Remain Flexible During Changes to Succeed

Success happens when you're clear on the end goal and flexible in how you'll get to that goal. A palm tree bends in hurricane force winds so it does not break and achieves the goal of surviving the storm. If you're too rigid and unwilling to bend or go with the flow when necessary then you're putting blocks in your own path. Be flexible but remain strong.

The same thing applies to change. Every moment of every day brings something new and different to experience. Sure it might feel like you're doing the same thing day after day at times but no two moments of your life are exactly the same. Being adaptable to change is key to being successful. Change brings opportunities. It's up to you to grab on to them when they come your way instead of letting them pass you by. Sometimes you will miss opportunities because you didn't recognize them as such. So it's very important to be aware of the doors and windows of change and opportunity opening and closing in your life.

The Law of Success applies to both negative and positive behavior. While it is my hope that you'll always strive for positivity, you can be successful with your negative behavior just as well as you can be successful with your positive behavior, however, the path is completely different. For example, let's say you're trying to get a specific job but there's someone ahead of you with more seniority who is next in line. If you take the positive approach and work hard to show upper management that you go above and beyond in your work then you may be offered the job, especially if the person above you doesn't really want it because it requires longer hours than they want to work. If someone took a negative approach that brought trouble to the person with the seniority, they'd probably still get the job but at what cost personally, spiritually, and at a soul level? If you take a negative approach to achieving success then you are creating karma (which is the Law of Karma) that will affect you in the form of debts that need to be repaid. But when you take a positive approach then you will receive karmic rewards. If you experience unexplained success that just seems to fall into your lap it is a karmic reward for the positivity you've shown in the past or in a past life.

Actions show everyone around you exactly the type of person you are on the inside. To be truly successful, treat people with dignity and respect, and always make sure you're walking the high road. Remember you are always compensated for everything you do.

The Law of Success also urges you to maintain an optimistic outlook. Look for the positive and pay it forward. See the glass as half full instead of half empty, know there are silver linings in every experience and situation, and see hope and possibilities all around you. Optimism can take you places and bring you success. Pessimism will hold you back. If you've fallen into the rut of pessimistic thinking, now is a great time to turn it around so you can see the awesome possibilities in your life.

Let Go of What Doesn't Help You

I make it a habit to clear out what no longer serves my greater good on a regular basis. This means if there are things that I'm putting my time and energy into but it's not bringing me the results I wanted to achieve, and I've given it my very best effort, then I let it go. If there are people who are bringing me down, who are not true friends but only want to use me, then I let them go. If something or someone is causing me too much stress, worry, or drama, I let it/them go. I prefer to move forward in life drama-free with as little stress as possible. It wasn't always this way though. In my youth, I thrived on drama. The more intense it was, the better I liked it. As I grew in my own spirituality and connected with my inner essence, I realized I was part of a whirlwind of emotional discord that caused me to be upset, stressed, or angry all the time and that it was very negative. I purposefully chose to let go of all the things causing me distress, and you know what happened? I felt more peaceful and calm than I had in years. Life will always throw some drama your way; it's how you choose to handle it that is important. When you eliminate the things that are no longer serving you, that aren't helping you to move forward to achieve what you want to achieve in life, then you clear the way for new opportunities and adventures.

When you're living the Law of Success you must be persistent in achieving your goals and never give up on them. Being persistent is necessary to your overall success. I've always been an avid reader and always had a long-term goal to be a multi-published author but I also enjoyed doing work to help authors. I've run several sites that promoted books or offered services to authors, all of which I let go because it took time away from my own writing. Now I write full time and only do pre-designed covers for other authors. I never gave up and was persistent in achieving my goal of being an author and of helping other authors. In order to get where I am today, I had to choose to let go of some of the things I enjoyed but that were holding me back from becoming a successful author. Each of these experiences had varying levels of success but were also stepping stones in getting me to where I am now. Take a look at your own stepping stones on your path to success to see how far you've come. How were you persistent? What did you let go of to move forward?

Try It Now

This is a quick and easy exercise that you can use to start each day. After you finish getting ready for the day and before you walk out the door go to a mirror and look into your eyes. See your inner essence, your true spiritual self, inside your body and say to yourself, "Today I will have a fantastic day. I will meet each challenge with a smile and take myself one step closer to everything I desire. I am a successful person on my way to achieving my goals." It's a great little pep talk to get you in an optimistic mood for the day.

Practical Application Tips

- Write down what success means to you. Review it often.

- Make a list of your goals and check it daily.

- Expect to be successful. If you expect it, you will attain it.

- Believe you will be successful and achieve your goals.

- Let go of that which no longer serves you. Clear out the old to make way for the new.

- Do not be afraid to fail. When you are courageous in your pursuits, fears fall behind you.

- Never give up on your ultimate goals.

- Work hard. Don't expect things to be handed to you but if they are, smile and say thank you to the universe for the karmic gift.

- Be flexible, strong, and persistent.

- Only you are responsible for your success. Don't blame lack of success on others. Get out there and make it happen!

See Also Chapter 34: The Law of Prosperity

17

THE LAW OF
RELATIVITY

— ✦ —

*Today I see myself as a positive, unique individual
striving to achieve the success I desire.*

THE LAW OF RELATIVITY, which was first introduced in scientific theory by Albert Einstein, states that everything in our physical world is made real by its relationship to something else. Until you compare two things they stand alone as separate entities. Once you compare two or more things, then they become relative to one another. That means that nothing is big or small until you relate it to something else. A ten-story building is just a ten-story building until compared to a three-story building—then it appears really tall. But a ten-story building compared to a sixty-story skyscraper makes the ten-story building appear very short. It's all relative. We give meaning in our own minds based on the comparisons we make. Otherwise it just exists as part of the whole.

The Law of Relativity means as spiritual beings we will all experience our own unique set of lessons that will increase our inner light. These lessons often present as tests or problems we have to solve. The Law of Relativity means regardless of how bad we perceive our situation, there is always someone who is having a more difficult time in life than we are *and* there are always people who are having a much easier time. Our lesson is to be able to become aware of these relative differences and act accordingly. When we compare our situations to others, it strengthens our ability to see life from different perspectives while learning to help ourselves and others based on these perspectives.

We know light exists because we compare it to darkness. In the physical world light translates into daytime and darkness into nighttime. In the spiritual world, we know that there is light within each of us because we see it in the good deeds performed by people every day but we also know there is darkness in each of us because we also see it through the negative actions of others. If the Law of Relativity didn't exist, then we'd never see the differences or be able to grow in our own spirituality. It's only in the earthly plane that we see differences in one another, because in the spiritual realm we are all one and the same, a part of the whole, pure light, pure goodness, and eternally at peace with one another. This is what we should also strive to achieve on the earthly plane.

When you think of the Law of Relativity and making comparisons, it's imperative that you position yourself within the comparison so you are elevating your self-esteem, remaining positive in your thoughts, and are lifting yourself out of negative patterns to be successful in attaining what you want in life. If you approach the Law of Relativity from the negative, you may achieve some success but it will often be a struggle and the ultimate goal may slip through your fingers. If you change your way of thinking from negative to positive, it will be easier to attain your ultimate goal.

Learning through Relativity

If everything is relative then how are you learning lessons? It is all based on your reactions to and actions taken in response to the tests you've been given. The more positive your reactions and actions the more you grow spiritually. If your reaction is negative or you have a poor, pitiful, why me, whining attitude which causes you to lash out at others or withdraw within yourself, then this is a negative response which will block your growth and your success. Each lesson will be one you wanted to learn prior to being born in the earthly plane of existence. Try to remember that all of your experiences are to bring you spiritual growth so you will have the proper reactions and take the needed action to achieve that growth.

When you're living the Law of Relativity you are giving the things in your life meaning. Without this law, life wouldn't have meaning. You would just exist, doing everything by rote, living without purpose, without goals, and life would be dull and mundane. But it does exist so you can set goals for yourself, strive to achieve these goals by comparing the steps you're taking to what other successful people have done.

It is important to remember not to use the Law of Relativity against yourself. If you compare yourself to someone who has become proficient at things while you're still learning or someone who is successful in a field you want to excel in, it's a good way to keep yourself motivated while reaching for your goal and striving to achieve the same level of success. If you compare yourself unfavorably to the person, you may think they've attained so much that you'll never be able to acquire the same level of success, and *then* you're making yourself look bad in your own eyes and will probably feel bad about yourself too. That's using the Law of Relativity incorrectly and is self-defeating. Don't make yourself miserable by using the law in a negative way.

Instead use the Law of Relativity to keep you motivated and on track to reach your goals, let it heighten your self-esteem. While the Law of Relativity indicates that you should compare yourself to others who haven't achieved what you've already achieved in order to make yourself look better, I would like to warn against this because you don't want to give yourself a superiority complex by thinking you're better than someone else. Comparison of this type can block your progress. Look at your own path and reach higher instead of looking down on others to make yourself feel better. Everyone does something better than someone else; we all have our gifts, talents, and abilities that make us the unique spiritual beings we are. When we understand and accept this, we're one step closer to living in harmony as one.

Compare, Don't Judge

The Law of Relativity isn't about judging other people. It's simply comparison. It's a way to notice the good in your life when you're feeling like things are going wrong. Whatever you're experiencing right now, no matter how bad or difficult you think your situation is it could always be worse. If you compare your situation to something worse, then the Law of Relativity can help you feel better about the situation and realize it isn't as bad as you originally thought. It allows you to see the situation differently based on the meaning you've given to the comparison you've made regarding your situation and another worse situation. If the comparison helps you feel better about your current situation, gives you a clearer picture, or adds more meaning to the way your life is progressing without being judgmental, you're using the law correctly.

When making comparisons to other people, it's important to remember that we are each unique individuals with different life plans. Each of our experiences are just as unique as we are on a spiritual level. These experiences add up to put us where we are right now, in this moment, on our life path. Maybe you want to be a champion skateboarder and are comparing yourself to someone who already has achieved that status. Don't let your falls get you down. The champion had to fall off the skateboard many times to develop the skills needed to become a winner. You can win too and the falls you experience only make your skill that much better. Be thankful for each slip off the board or every bumpy ride because those will enhance your ability and make your success spectacular when you achieve your goal.

Try It Now

Changing your frame of mind while using the Law of Relativity is very important, yet it's easy to remain stuck in your old ways and a negative mindset. Unless you change the way you think you can be easily frustrated or overwhelmed. So what you're going to do with this exercise is create a clean slate day. Pick a day on the calendar when you will let go of all negative thoughts and position yourself in a place of relativity that flows with your unique spiritual self and the personal desires you want to achieve. Once you pick a day, you're going to make a big deal about it every single morning beginning on day one. Now, take two jars and label one with a ☺ for positive actions/thoughts and the other with a for ☹ negative actions/thoughts. When you're getting ready for the day, look yourself in the eye and tell yourself that you're going to have a fantastic day full of positivity, fun, and achievements. Become very aware of your negative thinking so that you recognize it when it happens. Every time you catch yourself thinking or acting negatively, put a quarter in the ☹ jar. Then, each time you think or take positive action, take a quarter out of the ☹ jar and put it in the ☺ jar. Soon the ☺ jar will be overflowing and the ☹ jar will be empty.

Practical Application Tips
- Change your thoughts to enhance success.

- You can create your own relativity and success through thought, reaction, and action.

- Everything just is. The universe works in neutrality. How you see yourself in the grand scheme of life is directly proportionate to the success you will attain.

- See yourself as having, being, and achieving your desires to ensure success.

- Use the Law of Relativity to empower you at a soul level.

- Keep self-sabotage to a minimum by using the Law of Relativity to lift yourself up instead of feeling that you'll never achieve your goals.

- Use the Law of Relativity not to compare yourself to another person but to compare paths to reaching similar goals.

- Use the Law of Relativity to support your goals, desires, and dreams through positive evaluations.

- Remember things could always be worse and they can always be better. Use where you are now as a stepping stone in relation to where you want to be. Step forward and up, not backward and down.

- Simply compare—do not judge.

See Also Chapter 2: The Law of Divine Oneness

18

THE LAW OF CORRESPONDENCE

— 🕊 —

Today I create my own reality based on the
beliefs within me. I will shine and excel in joy.

THE LAW OF CORRESPONDENCE states that the laws of the physical world regarding motion, light, vibration, and other scientific ideals have a corresponding law in the spiritual universe. The Law of Correspondence is stated in the *Kybalion* as "As above, so below; as below, so above." It is also often stated as "As within, so without" and in the shortened version of "As above, so below." What, exactly, does this mean?

As Within, So Without

As within, so without means that how you feel inside, at your true spiritual core, your beliefs and thoughts, are directly reflected on the outside through your actions and behavior and will absolutely affect your experiences in this realm of existence on the earthly plane. That is why, in order to be successful, you must make sure your inner world is running smoothly, without drama, with positive intent, and is abundant in happiness and joy because those are the things you would want to experience in your physical reality. If your inner world is in a state of constant unrest, with too much drama, worry, and continuous struggles, then that's what you'll experience in the physical. Because your inner life is reflected into your outer life, you must take care of your emotions, thoughts, and how you look at the physical world. If these are out of balance, then your physical reality, including the relationships you have with other people, your career, the amount of money you'll be able to make, how much you'll be able to prosper and succeed in life, all of these things will be out of balance as well.

If you notice you're experiencing a lot of negativity in your physical world, then there is negativity within you. The Law of Correspondence helps you find inner negativity so you can eliminate it once and for all. You may have buried negative feelings like anger, jealousy, or fear so deep that you're denying it even to yourself. This is when you need to uncover every nuance of negativity within so what is reflected without is positive. Think of it as spiritual spring cleaning. Once you do this, you'll see changes in your external environment. If you had a fear of people leaving you, now they no longer leave but instead stay a part of your life. If you had been holding anger inside, people no longer take their anger out on you but are pleasant. If you let go of your lack of trust in others, now you'll find people are more trusting of you. When you change yourself, others change to mirror your internal changes. What you believe is reflected into the universe and your physical reality so make sure you believe in your utmost success.

As Above, So Below

As above, so below. This means that the physical world corresponds to the spiritual world and the universe. There are many layers of existence, such as the spiritual universe, that we are unable to see and are unknown to us except through the Law of Correspondence. This law allows us to achieve harmony through understanding and receiving spiritual truths between the spiritual realm and the earthly plane of existence. In essence this means the spiritual realm is mirrored in the physical realm. Many religions have the ideal of *on Earth as it is in heaven* which is a reflection of the Law of Correspondence. Consider for a moment the amount of love and positive energy in the spiritual realm. This directly corresponds with the amount of love you feel in your heart for the world around you, the people in your life, and the things you enjoy doing. Since you are part of the whole, then it's easy to see the connection between the spiritual realm *above* and yourself living on the physical realm *below*.

In the spiritual realm, we are each responsible for our unique essence. We are there for one another but we are not responsible for each other's path. Every entity's path is uniquely their own. It's the same below. You are not responsible for the path of anyone else. You can offer assistance and guide others, but ultimately they will make their own decisions that will affect their path. You are only responsible for your own path and spiritual growth. While you may want to try to help someone who is going down the wrong path, the only thing you truly have control over is your own self, the way you feel, how you think, and the things you do in life.

If you feel stuck in a rut and don't know what to do to change yourself the first thing you must do is take responsibility for your actions. If you're wrong, admit it to yourself. You don't have to admit it to anyone else right now, although you might want to later, but you have to be honest with yourself. It's really easy to claim responsibility when things are great, but what about when you do something wrong? Are you putting blame on others when the fault is really yours? It's easy to lay blame elsewhere and hard to accept when you're in the wrong. But the more you accept responsibility for what you're doing, thinking, saying, and feeling, the easier it will become. Make a thorough examination of your life. Look at where you've been and where you're going. Think about how your thoughts and actions have affected your path up until now. Do you see a pattern? Is it positive or negative? Do you need to change your attitude, work ethic, or anything else to obtain a different outcome? If you do, start today to make changes internally so they will affect you positively externally. You can have anything you desire in life but you have to want it and make the changes necessary to achieve it.

Every situation is an opportunity to learn something new about yourself. If you do then you're continually growing and moving forward, which is part of the purpose of being. It's your job to make sure you're taking advantage of every opportunity to learn. Life isn't sugar-coated. You must take the good with the bad and learn from both. *As above*, God, the Source, the universe, whatever you call the higher power of creation, wants you to succeed and obtain all that your heart desires, but *as below*, it's your responsibility to make things happen with the gifts you've been given. I always say the universe works on its own timetable; the things we wanted yesterday will come when the time is right. You can't force things to happen *right now*, but you can change within *right now*. It's all up to you.

Déjà vu and Synchronicity

Have you ever experienced déjà vu? Have you experienced a really weird coincidence? How about synchronicity, when things happen and seem complexly intertwined but aren't connected? That's a message from above for you to pay more attention to what's going on in your life. To me, déjà vu is an indication that you're on the right path. It is a sign your Divine self planned while still in the spiritual realm to let you know you're going in the right direction. The more often and powerful the déjà vu, the more potent the message to keep going forward because what you seek is right around the corner. I personally don't believe in coincidences. I believe everything happens for a reason even if we don't know the reason at the point in time when we have the experience. Sometimes the reason will become known later and other times you'll find it out when you're back on the spiritual plane. When you pay attention to the signs that are being sent to you, then you are opening your awareness and making it easier to obtain success and achieve your desires. When you ignore these messages then you are missing opportunities that would enable you to obtain what you want faster. Living life with your eyes wide open can allow you to expect the unexpected, to believe in the unbelievable, and attain what may seem unattainable.

Try It Now

This is a difficult exercise but it's one I want you to really think about while being utterly, brutally, and completely honest with yourself. Choose one thing you want to achieve. Is it a loving relationship, a home, a vehicle, wealth, more happiness in your life, or a physical object? I want you to make a list of the things you do that are holding you back from achieving your desires. Is it your attitude? If so, what aspect of your attitude is holding you back? Are you angry, jealous, overly competitive, feeling undeserving, or are you trying so hard to please others that you're not following your own dreams? List everything you can think of inside you that is keeping you from achieving your goal and moving forward. Don't write down anything about anyone else, and don't place blame on anyone else. If you feel the need to place blame, look deep within and discover what is inside of you that deserves the blame. Once you have your list complete, I want you to write beside each item a positive action you can take to change what's holding you back so you begin to move forward. Evaluate this list regularly, and do the exercise over from time to time. By being aware of what's inside, you can change and create a new reality for yourself.

Practical Application Tips

- Take responsibility for yourself, your thoughts, and your actions.

- Don't place blame on others.

- Be honest with yourself. This is your life, your path.

- Realize you can't change others or be responsible for their paths.

- Connect with the flow of universal energy to reap the rewards you seek.

- If you're stuck in a rut, take action to make changes within to see results without.

- Use the Law of Correspondence to gain knowledge from the unknown.

- Expect the unexpected.

- Give of yourself unconditionally.

- Only you can change the direction your life is taking. Set your sights high and go for your dreams.

See Also Chapter 20: The Law of Cooperation

19

THE LAW OF COMPENSATION

— 🕊 —

As I give, I will receive, be it today,
tomorrow, or at some time in the future.

THE LAW OF COMPENSATION states that you will always be paid for
the energy you have expended by receiving energy back from the universe tenfold. This is also known as the Law of Karma which first appeared in the ancient Hindu *Rigveda*. Even if you're not expecting to
receive anything for your deeds, or even if you don't want to receive
anything back for what you've done, the universe will still compen-
sate you for the energy you've given out, whether it's positive or negative…and whether you want it or not.

Think of this law as a vast circle. When you expend energy outward, it affects another person who receives your energy, which allows
them to give energy in turn to someone else until the energy comes

back around to you. The person who receives your energy is doing so in order for you to be compensated for giving it. It may come back to you in the form of love, money, relationships, material items, happiness, joy, or blessings. To prevent negative energy from coming back to you, try to always send out positive energy. Have you ever heard the saying, *what goes around comes around*? This saying is usually used when discussing karma but it can also be used to discuss the Law of Compensation. The energy you receive back can be thought of as consequences of your actions. It could happen instantly, in a few days, months or years, or it could happen in your next lifetime. There is no time limit on when the Law of Compensation will pay you back for the deeds you've done but you will be paid for them.

If you feel as if there isn't enough abundance to go around, you may also feel that you shouldn't receive anything back for the good deeds you're doing, then you're setting up a road block not only for yourself but also for those receiving your energy. The energy flows in a circular manner, so you must receive energy back once you give it out. When you tell others not to worry about compensating you, then you've clogged the free flow of energy. A good example of this is how you handle compliments. Many people aren't comfortable receiving compliments from others. While the giver of the compliment is giving out positive energy, when you don't readily accept the compliment, you're blocking the energy so that it has a harder time returning to the person who sent it to you.

Abundance Is Infinite

The abundance in the universe will never run out. There's enough for everyone in existence and then there's more after that. Abundance is readily available for you if you want it. The universe wants you to have as much as you need and then some. If you were to ask the universe for something to drink and brought a thimble, then that thimble would be filled. If you brought a swimming pool, that would be filled too. It doesn't matter how much you need or want, you'll always be able to receive all you ask for and more. The more you give, the more you receive in return.

The Law of Compensation urges us to increase our ability to give and receive. It encourages us to offer praise more often and complain less, to pay for what we receive either with money or in return kindnesses, and to look at the role of others when it comes to compensation. When you're living the Law of Compensation try not to lay blame on others. Own up to your actions and if you don't like what you're seeing, then make changes. Changes in your reality helps you recognize the effects that the Law of Compensation has on you at a spiritual level.

Most people think of money when they consider the Law of Compensation simply because compensation means to be paid. While the law is much more than finances, let's look at the law in regard to money for a moment. In addition to spiritual giving and receiving, this law can help you understand and handle financial matters and material gains by opening your eyes more fully to the consequences of investments and charitable donations and how you spend, save, and manage your money.

Financial Compensation

For the Law of Compensation to work for you financially, you must first examine the way you think about money. Do you think of your financial state from a place of lack or abundance? If you're stuck in a lack mentality, you're unconsciously giving out the energy of lack. In turn you get back the same, keeping you from getting ahead financially. To break this cycle, think back to discover why you are thinking this way.

Consider how you handle money. Do you count every penny without ever giving any away? If you are, you could be causing unnecessary blocks. When you give more, you get more in return. This is true whether you're talking about money, emotions, thoughts, or the things you say to yourself and others. This doesn't mean to be irresponsible with your money, but not to hoard it, instead, give some just to give. I once knew a man who would pay for his meals and leave the change sitting on the tray. When he threw out his trash, he threw the change out too. That's one way you can let go of money but it doesn't help anyone sitting at the bottom of a trash bag. A way for him to help would have been to leave it as a gift on the table for whoever sat there next. Giving money away, or buying things with your money and then giving those things away to reputable causes or someone in need, is a way to help bring abundance into your life and it makes you feel good about yourself.

The Law of Compensation doesn't mean you'll get exactly what you give. For instance, if you volunteered to help someone move, they may not help you move in the future but they may show up on your doorstep the following week to take you out to dinner for helping them. You've received something back for your good deed when it wasn't expected. That's the Law of Compensation at work. Living the Law of Compensation requires patience. You know the saying; *good things come to those that wait*? That applies to this law. You may have to wait, but you will be compensated for your thoughts, feelings, and actions.

Compensating Yourself

Do you give to yourself? Or are you always giving of yourself to others? With the Law of Compensation it's just as vitally important to give to yourself as it is to give of yourself. There has to be balance. When you give to yourself you are expressing love for yourself and a deep connection to your soul. Instead of creating lack for yourself because you're always giving of yourself to others, make sure you take the time to do things that are gifts to yourself. If you need to relax, take a spa day. If you want to boost your self-esteem get a haircut, have a manicure, or go work out in the gym. When you give to yourself you're recognizing, appreciating, and embracing your spiritual essence, which increases your feelings of self-worth and raises your spiritual frequency. You're creating a balance in your own energy by giving yourself as much importance as you give others. Treating yourself as you would treat others ensures positive energy coming back to you.

Always remember to be honest and positive in your giving. If you give for the wrong reasons or because you're expecting something in return for your gift, then you're setting yourself up to receive negativity back. Give from the heart, with love, and for the sake of helping others and yourself. Then you can receive an unlimited amount of abundance from the universe as a reward for living the Law of Compensation.

Try It Now

For this exercise I would like for you to give something from your heart to another person. You may lend a helping hand, give emotional support, or donate your time to a good cause. Give because you want to, not because you expect something back. Keep a journal of the positive things that happen to you, especially the unexpected. They can be little things like someone holding a door open for you or big things like someone helping you with a difficult situation at your job. Whatever you experience, write it down. This makes you more aware of the energy flowing back to you. This can help you get a handle on how the Law of Compensation is working in your life. This isn't meant to be a long-term journal, nor are you meant to keep score. It's simply a guide to get you on the right track until giving and receiving with ease becomes second nature to you.

Practical Application Tips

- You will receive compensation for the energy you give out so make it positive instead of negative.

- Learn to gracefully accept what you receive instead of denying it so the flow of energy isn't blocked.

- Give for the right reasons, not because you want something in return.

- Don't deny yourself universal abundance because you feel there isn't enough to go around.

- Examine your thoughts to make sure you're not inadvertently holding onto negative thought patterns that can adversely affect the energy coming back to you.

- The more you give the more you will receive.

- If your cup is running over with abundance, get a bigger cup so you can accept more of what the universe is offering you.

- The universe believes you're entitled to be compensated for the energy you expend and will give it back to you some way, somehow, whether you want it or not.

- Choose to send out positive energy so you'll get it in return.

- If you're having problems with giving or receiving, look inside yourself for the reasons and examine your feelings concerning both. Bring yourself into balance to live in harmony with the Law of Compensation.

See Also Chapter 8: The Law of Abundance

20

THE LAW OF COOPERATION

— 🕊 —

*Today I will make the best of every
experience I have through cooperation with
myself, the Divine, and the people I encounter.*

THE LAW OF COOPERATION means as a spiritual being you are in cooperation with yourself, the Divine, and others so that you may grow and learn on the earthly plane of existence. Cooperation with the Divine in order to achieve spiritual growth has been a fundamental part of many religions since ancient times just as it is today, and most often means setting aside the ego so the Divine can work through you to make your life and the world a better place. It means to make the best of what you're given without complaint or to take action to bring change.

By definition, cooperation means to work together to achieve the same results. We cooperate with people every day at our job, in random encounters, and any time we're trying to achieve a common goal. Living the Law of Cooperation means to take our responsibilities seriously and reach out to help others achieve their goals. This applies to teaching others, following your own path, and expanding your knowledge of the Divine.

The Law of Cooperation means you'll be presented with and will encounter many opportunities in your daily life where you can choose to be cooperative. There are three main areas where the Law of Cooperation helps you move forward on your spiritual path and bring you the results you're trying to achieve. The first is when you cooperate with yourself, the second is when you cooperate with the Divine, and the third is when you cooperate with others. Let's look at each of these areas in depth.

Cooperating with Yourself

Sometimes we can be our own worst enemies. We can expend a lot of energy trying to fight the hand life has dealt us or we can go with the universal flow of life and use our energy to cooperate and accept the situation, then make choices that will bring about positive change. You know the saying, *when life gives you lemons then make lemonade*? Well, it's the same idea. You can use up all of your energy fighting, arguing, or complaining about the situations you find yourself in or you can think of the best approach to use what you have been given or to do something about changing the situation to suit your needs. Decide what each situation is teaching you. When you learn something you grow spiritually and often realize new information from the lesson that will help you achieve your goals. Then take action, based on the lesson, to get you moving in a forward direction through cooperating with yourself instead of thinking you've been blocked and will never be able to obtain what you want because of that block. There are always ways to get over, around, and through blocks, you just have to be cooperative to find them. Don't deny the blocks you encounter because that will only make you defensive. Instead acknowledge the situation, cooperate within yourself, work through the blocks, and work with the universe in order to accept the situation and move forward from it to future goals.

Cooperating with the Divine

One of the ways we cooperate with the Divine is to teach others by sharing our experiences. We are cooperating with our master plan which was created when we were still on the other side. Through teaching, not only do we get to know our own spiritual selves better because to be a teacher you must always continue to learn, but we also are able to help others along their spiritual path by providing information that will enable them to become more enlightened.

There are other ways we can cooperate with the Divine. When you encounter a situation, whether it's positive or negative, do everything you can to make the situation work out in the best possible way. It may not be your lesson to find the solution but the lesson of another and your role is to cooperate with them to achieve the desired results. One of the hardest ways of cooperating with the Divine is in letting go. As human beings we like to remain in control. When you let go of something, or someone, you're not losing out, instead you're allowing the person or situation and yourself the freedom to cooperate with the universe. It's part of the ebb and flow of universal energy. When you release something you also have to release the worry that may have been associated with it. Worrying about something isn't going to change the outcome and it's a negative trait that can block you.

When you're cooperating with the Divine, be flexible. Think of trees during a storm. The flexible trees will bend and the rigid ones will break. Through cooperation with the Divine you ensure you're bending and not breaking when you encounter difficulties. The Divine wants you to succeed and master the lessons you've been sent here to learn. Make the best of the things happening to you, go with the flow, and be prepared for the unexpected. That doesn't mean you're always waiting for the next bad thing to happen, that's counterproductive and isn't being cooperative. If you're always waiting for something negative, you can't enjoy the positive as it happens. Instead, let it go and live in the now.

Cooperating with Other People

There are many times when you will need to work with other people in order to achieve a common goal. You will often encounter this at your job. All work is related to achieving a common goal and achieving the same end result. For instance, let's say you work in a supermarket. Your job as a cashier is to make sure that the customers are checked out in a timely manner and they have a great shopping experience at the supermarket. In order for the supermarket to function, you also have a manager, shelf stockers, produce managers, deli workers, bakery workers, baggers, order pickers, and others who are all working in cooperation to make sure the entire facility runs smoothly with great customer service so it stays in business by earning a profit. Each job is just as important as another in the overall function of the supermarket. I'm sure at some point you've worked with or encountered an employee who was argumentative, disruptive, and uncooperative with others, including customers. While that person is in the workplace, it causes everyone else to be on edge, but when they are gone, harmony returns. When you're cooperative, you are working in harmony with others. You'll also find yourself cooperating with people in other areas too. Maybe someone's car broke down and you decide to help out by helping to push it out of the road or you're leaving a store at the same time as someone else and you hold the door open for them. These are little ways you're helpful but also cooperating with someone at a given moment in time to achieve the same result. If you look at each experience to see what you're learning from it, then you're living the Law of Cooperation.

There are some important characteristics to strive for when cooperating with others. Listen to what others are saying and make sure you understand exactly what needs to be done to achieve a desired goal. Share your own ideas, abilities, and time to reach the goal. If there is someone just as qualified to do a job as you are, choose to do something else and let them have their turn. When you do your part, or if you compromise in times of conflict, it shows others you are being a cooperative team player which will encourage them to do the same. Show your appreciation for the work and cooperation others are also giving to the end goal. When others are acknowledged for positive action and encouraged to keep doing a great job then it strengthens the bond between everyone who is cooperating to reach a goal because each person feels needed. Encourage others along the way to make reaching an end result uplifting and fun.

The Law of Cooperation urges you to have faith that the situations you experience will be beneficial to you in the long run. These experiences will help you grow in Spirit. Whatever you really want in life, the Law of Cooperation will help you attain it, but you must do your part. Begin cooperating now to ensure your life is successful, happy, and filled with abundance.

Try It Now

How could cooperation help you attain a goal? If you asked other people to help you, could you reach your goal faster? What would be the consequences of asking for help? Would the other people be able to have an experience they'll always remember? Would they receive something in exchange for helping you? Or is this goal something you need to do personally and alone. If it is, how can you achieve it by being more cooperative with yourself and the Divine? Keep a journal of this exercise and how long it takes you to attain this goal. Make note of how being cooperative made a difference.

Practical Application Tips

- Try to refrain from creating unnecessary drama for yourself.

- Learn to let go.

- Acknowledge others and the job they are doing.

- Work together with yourself, the universe and other people to create an environment of positive cooperation that flows in forward motion.

- Accept that other people may be better qualified to do something than you are and let them do it. You're better at something else and will be needed in that area. Believe you will reach your goals when you cooperate.

- Bend, don't break.

- If a situation seems unfair, look at it from a neutral perspective. Are you reading more into it than is there? If you are, then you're not cooperating with yourself. Let it go to bring yourself back into balance.

- Cooperation allows everyone to shine, to have their needs met, and to offer experiences and lessons that wouldn't be available otherwise.

- Cooperation isn't about being passive and letting others do everything. It's being fully engaged and responsible for your actions and willingly working toward the same goal.

See Also Chapter 18: The Law of Correspondence

21

THE LAW OF PERSPECTIVE

— 🕊 —

Today I see from here to there, up and down,
forward and backward, so that my point
of view is ever changing and never stagnant.

THE LAW OF PERSPECTIVE states that every person has a unique point of view or attitude which is relative to their personal belief. As belief changes, perspective changes. Life is how you perceive it. Saint Thomas Aquinas's stated that anyone could decide what is truth and that they didn't have to do something if they felt it went against natural law. At the time this was a liberating idea on many levels for the people. It indicated that a person's perspective determined their own truth.

How you perceive your experiences is important when examining your life. Your perspective determines how you think about something, your reaction to it, and whether you will take action for or against it.

Perspective affects your reality every single day. It gives you the opportunity to choose to be positive or negative in your actions based on how you perceive situations. Your perspective affects your emotions. It makes you look forward to an event, or dread it. You can be excited, enthusiastic, or over the moon about a relationship, or you can be distrustful, pessimistic, or simply over it. Perspective can make you curious, engaging, fearful, delighted, competitive, compassionate, and generally affects every human emotion and determines the emotions you feel towards situations and other people.

The key to using perspective to get what you want in life is to use it to see multiple points of view. It's putting yourself in someone else's shoes, it's thinking out of the box, and it's changing your thoughts to change your reality. It's using perspective to put yourself in the driver's seat and taking charge of your life instead of riding along as a passenger watching the scenery go by. It's expanding your world view to encompass more information. Perspective can help you during difficult times or when you feel like you can't move forward in life. Contemplating how to get unstuck from a different perspective offers new ideas that can propel you out of the rut and into a higher frequency where you welcome change to get you going again.

Your level of consciousness and your connection to your spiritual self determines how your experiences will happen every single day. If you're in an upbeat mood you will tend to see things in a positive manner which will make your day flow easily and with less stress. But if you've had lack of sleep, are overwhelmed, stressed or exhausted, then these will factor into your perspective and can make things that would otherwise be positive, seem negative. Your perspective changes from day to day based upon external factors. If you're doing too much and not getting enough rest, then you need to make changes so you have less on your plate and are able to get enough sleep. When you're tired, molehills can become mountains and a glass will seem half-empty instead of half-full. It's all about perspective. Doing something spontaneous and unexpected can help jumpstart a positive mindset, which will change your negative perspective back to a positive one.

Time, Love, and Perspective

Your perspective also affects time. Have you ever noticed when you're excited about something and can't wait for it to happen that it seems to take forever for the day to arrive, yet when you're under a deadline and have to get something done but keep getting interrupted, time just seems to fly by? It's the same way when you're doing things you enjoy. You can get lost in a project you love only to discover the whole day has passed by and you were so engrossed in what you were doing that you forgot to eat. But if it's a task you're not looking forward to or you don't enjoy then you're looking at the clock every five minutes and the day just seems to drag by. What would happen if you changed your perspective? Could you make your boring day go by faster by thinking of a reward you'll give yourself after work?

If you look at life from the perspective of love you can gain more understanding for others because it enables you to identify with their position, point of view, and their perspective. You don't necessarily have to agree with them but looking past your own perspective to consider and understand that of another person allows insight into their thought processes and the reasons for their actions and behaviors. In business, this is helpful because, when you understand others, it is easier to work as a team to reach common goals or gain insight into your competition. By understanding their perspective you can see where they've been and where they plan to go strategically and this can help you move forward by favorably altering the way you act and respond to them once you understand them better.

If you're trying to become more financially wealthy, when you understand the perspective and the pathways chosen by those who are already wealthy, then it shows you a path you can follow that has already been successful. Even slight shifts in your perspective can open doors you may have thought were closed to you. How you look at things can often bring about opportunities you may not have known existed from your previous viewpoint.

Goal Setting and Plans

The Law of Perspective can also affect your goal setting and plans. When I was in college I wanted to be a model and actress so I obtained my degree in theater. I modeled during college and afterwards obtained some acting jobs but never really did much else with my degree. Doing so, however, gave me insight into people I wouldn't have had otherwise. As an actress I had to develop characters and understand what motivated that character to do the things she did. This enabled me to take a different perspective from my own. When I began writing fiction, my degree in theater was very valuable in helping me to create characters for my books that were believable and well rounded. My goals and plans changed after college, which altered my perspective at that time, but the experiences I had came back to help me with character development in my novels (this doesn't apply to my nonfiction books). When you're making plans and setting goals for yourself, don't write them in stone so that they never change. As you meet new people and have new experiences you may change your perspective often, which can alter your plans. If you expect change then you'll never be caught unaware. Everything changes; something you thought was bad yesterday might be great today based on new knowledge you obtained. If you're able to go with the flow of life with a changing perspective then you'll experience less stress and more success.

The Law of Perspective also means having an understanding of what is important in your life. You're able to find ways to compromise to be successful and happy in what you enjoy doing and the plans you have made. It means asking others how they see a situation so you can understand their perspective without passing judgment or getting defensive. It's being flexible, learning, compromising, encouraging, and helping other people because sometimes their success helps you to become more successful.

As you're reaching toward your goals always remember to be in tune with your perspective. If you're positive and optimistic you'll see things in a clearer light than if you're in a bad mood. Sometimes problems that seem unsolvable in the middle of the night have clear solutions during the light of day. It's due to the change in perspective. This can also mean that negativity is surrounded by darkness but positivity is found in the light because you're seeing the situation from a different point of view. Let your own light shine in the darkness to erase negativity and find a new perspective on your life, goals, and path to success.

Try It Now

Here's a fun exercise to examine your perspective. Get a glass of water and a package of food coloring that has blue, red, yellow and green in it. Fill the glass half way with water and set it on a table. Put a piece of paper and pen beside it so you can take notes about what you see and how you feel about it. Now, from your perspective do you see the glass as half-full or half-empty? Why? Write it down. Now choose one of the four food color bottles and put one drop into the glass of water. How does adding one drop of color change your perspective? Keep adding drops, making notes of what you think of the water as it changes colors. When the glass contained only water did you think of it as clear, refreshing, or pure? As you added color did it become bright, vibrant, or murky? As you complete this exercise, examine how subtle changes of color can completely alter your perspective of the water.

Practical Application Tips

- To change your perspective, step into someone else's shoes for a moment to see things from their point of view.

- Your level of consciousness affects your perspective and the actions you take in any given situation.

- To increase your ability to view a situation from multiple perspectives, increase your spiritual frequency.

- If you find yourself judging others instead of trying to see their point of view, it's time to examine your own perspective.

- Success is found through compromise, encouragement, flexibility, and continually seeking to understand what you may not know.

- Lack of sleep, being overly stressed, or feeling overwhelmed by life can lead to a limited perspective. Make sure you're getting enough rest and aren't overdoing it so you can see with clarity.

- To make time go faster or slower, change your perception of it.

- A new perspective can enable you to be creative, spontaneous, and successful.

- If you're not sure why someone has a certain point of view, ask. It will help you understand one another better. You may not agree, but sometimes you have to agree to disagree.

- Look for the silver lining in everything.

See Also Chapter 22: The Law of Thought

22

THE LAW OF THOUGHT

— 🕊 —

My thoughts are positive, harmonious, and powerful.
They guide me to achieve my goals and enable me to
create strength of character to help myself and others.

THE LAW OF THOUGHT means that your state of mind, positive or negative, is reflected in your external reality. Thoughts are made of energy that can be targeted toward a specific outcome. This means to change your state of mind is to change your reality. If you don't like how your life is going, take charge of your thoughts and change directions to a path of prosperity and happiness. Philosophers such as Plato, Aristotle, Heraclitus, and Parmenides of Elea had theories about the Laws of Thought that were based on contradiction and non-contradiction and were often a source of great debate. Heraclitus believed that things changed so they must already contain what they would change into, whereas Aristotle believed that nothing could exist and not exist at the same time. If you apply these two theories to New Age spirituality, you already have whatever you want to be within you and negativity can't exist when there's positivity.

I've always believed thoughts are living things you send out into the world to do your bidding so you can accomplish what you want to achieve. Thought is an unbelievably powerful force that can create, heal, and change lives. I always try to keep my thoughts positive and never think of things I wouldn't want to happen. When you speak your thoughts aloud, you give them even more power to accomplish what you want and those thoughts will eventually manifest in your life. Your intention behind your thoughts is also very important so choose a positive intent when living the Law of Thought.

Comparison and Contrasting Thoughts

When I'm writing, I teach by comparing and contrasting positives and negatives, which isn't the same as sitting here thinking of doom and gloom or bad things. The difference is that when I discuss something less than positive in my books, it helps the reader recognize something they may be doing that hadn't occurred to them before that moment. It provides multiple perspectives while learning about the topic. If the reader sees something in themselves they can change, then the contrast worked as a teaching tool.

Consciously controlling negative thought behavior means being aware of negative thoughts that don't have your best interest at heart when you think them. If you lapse and think negatively, counteract it with a positive thought as an attempt to keep the negative thought from manifesting. If you run into problems or negativity, step away from the situation, run through possible positive scenarios in your mind on how to resolve the issue, and come back to it in a little while. Refreshing yourself will enable you to see the positive in a negative situation. Oftentimes when you return to the situation, you will see it in a new light or it will have resolved on its own accord. Never try to resolve negative issues with negativity. That will always backfire, create frustration, and opposition from others involved. It's best to step away than to get into an argument or fight over something that can be resolved in other ways.

Be Aware to Maintain Forward Movement

The Law of Thought urges you to always be aware of your current mind-set as well as your emotions at any given time. If you're upset it's easy to fall back into negative thinking and actions, which you'll probably regret when your emotions have returned to their normal positivity. To get over any of these negative feelings, do something! If you're tired, rest. If you're irritated, frustrated, or bored, take a walk, ride your bike, or do anything to get your body energized. When you're filled with physical energy you'll be more positive and energetic. You are not just a product of your circumstances. If you desire to have different conditions in your life, you can achieve them by changing your state of mind to create the life that you want. Your thoughts are creating your external world. Things are not happening to you, but you are manifesting them in your life due to your thoughts. You're responsible for the life you create for yourself and the experiences you have along the way. No one else can change your life for you; it's something you have to be willing to do for yourself. Once you make the decision and start changing your thoughts, don't look back—move forward with strength and determination that you will be successful in everything you do.

Positive thoughts can help you build a strong character. Your state of mind, morals, and intention in life are what will make you stand out as a trustworthy person who does the right thing. When you think of yourself as strong in every area of your life, then that strength radiates outward to affect those around you. When you have a positive effect on other people, it makes them want to be around you more. They respect you and want to see you do well in life.

The Chatterbox in Your Mind

We can't discuss the Law of Thought without discussing the inner chatterbox that likes to talk constantly in your mind expressing self doubt or jumping from one thought to another, rehashing situations you've experienced during the day with multiple alternate endings. It can make you think about what you should have said, action you should have taken, or how you would have handled the situation differently if you'd been given enough time to mull it over in your mind. Unless controlled, this inner chatterbox can create inconsistent thoughts, make you second guess yourself, and it will often wander about aimlessly until it finds another topic to discuss in your mind. This inner talk is mental noise that can keep you in a state of distracted frustration if you let it. Once a situation has happened, the best way to handle it is through acceptance and moving forward instead of rehashing it in your mind. The Law of Thought means to take the time to quiet your mind. If you're mind is going a mile a minute because of inner talk and you're thinking about everything under the sun, you will lose focus, making it easier for negativity to sneak in.

Training your mind to think good thoughts instead of negative ones will take a little time. The subconscious mind can be resistant to change but if you keep at it you will succeed and soon you'll consistently be thinking positive, good thoughts. Clear your thoughts by thinking of something that relaxes or inspires you. When you fill your mind with one thing that you enjoy, everything else just drifts away and quiets down. Another way to focus on positive thoughts is to think of your spiritual frequency. Feel the purity of your being, let the energy of your soul essence wash over you, releasing any negative thoughts you're holding onto. Feel yourself become lighter in Spirit and filled with the positivity of your soul. The more you can quiet your mind, retain good thoughts and release negative ones, the more peaceful, balanced, and harmonious you'll feel.

Going after your dreams requires positivity and focus. If your mind isn't cooperating with you because negativity is slipping in or because there's constant self-talk going on, then how can you remain focused on your goal? Thoughts are constantly in motion; they can create miracles that will dramatically change your life for the better if you're actively trying to make your thoughts more powerful, positive, and pure. Your thoughts are part of the universal stream of consciousness. That's why you are able to come up with unique ideas and ways of doing things. Consider that your thoughts are Divine, dynamic, and sustainable. If a thought doesn't fit these criteria, then let it go. Negative thoughts may not give up without a fight, but you are master of your mind, and it is your choice which thoughts stay and which ones go. You will prevail and find harmony in your mind through positive thoughts which will change your life.

Try It Now

I use this exercise to shut that little chatterbox up and quiet my mind. See if this exercise works for you. I imagine doors in my mind. Behind each door is a little room with shelves. I name each door accordingly as family, kid activities, the house, horses, writing, and *get out*. When I think of something that I can't address at the moment, I mentally imagine opening the appropriate door in my mind and putting the thought on the shelf for the time being. Later, when I have time, I open the door and address what I put inside. The door labeled *get out* is where I put those sneaky negative thoughts that I want to get completely out of my mind. Behind that door I imagine space with lots of stars. When I put a negative thought behind that door, it travels out into space to become a brightly shining star. Occasionally I'll open that door just to consider the many stars shining back at me. That's how many negative thoughts I've sent on their way to become something beautiful, bright, and filled with light.

Practical Application Tips

- Become aware of your current mindset.

- Release negative thoughts that will hold you back from achieving your dreams.

- Expect your mind to keep the negative chatter going until you've had enough practice that you can immediately cast out negative thoughts and replace them with positive thoughts.

- Thought is a Divine part of universal consciousness. Let it empower you.

- Control negative thought behavior though practice.

- Quiet the endless chatter of your mind by thinking of one thing, place, person, or event that inspires you.

- Change your thoughts to change the circumstances of your life.

- Thoughts are powerful, living things that can help you achieve your goals.

- Give your thoughts a task, send it out into the universe and enjoy the benefits it brings back to you.

- Thoughts create what they are. Think positive thoughts to move ahead in life and work through negative thoughts so you can let them go; this way they don't adversely affect you.

See Also Chapter 21: The Law of Perspective

23

THE LAW OF PASSIVITY

— 🕊 —

I am an active participant in my life.
I am in the driver's seat. I will take
charge of myself and be all that I am.

THE LAW OF PASSIVITY means that there are times in your life when you do not need to respond or take action, yet there are other times when taking an active role and making decisions is exactly what you need to do. The idea of passivity became important in philosophy after Aristotle included it in his list of categories. In *On the Soul* Aristotle said, "And in fact mind as we have described what it is by virtue of becoming all things, while there is another which is what it is by virtue of making all things: this is a sort of positive state like light; for in a sense light makes potential colors into actual colors. Mind in this sense of it is separable, impassible, unmixed, since it is in its essential nature activity (for always the active is superior to the passive factor, the originating force to the matter which it forms)." The Law of Passivity means to fully commit to the things you want to achieve instead of waiting for them to come to you. It is finding balance between passivity and activity. When you're too passive, you're more attached to lack instead of actively trying to bring about the changes needed to achieve your goals. Likewise if you're too active and forceful, then you may become too aggressive.

When you have a passive mindset, you may do anything possible to avoid conflict, go along with the crowd or what someone else wants to do instead of voicing your desires, or you may blame yourself when things go wrong instead of seeing where the blame truly lies. You may keep to yourself, hold your feelings inside, and never let your desires or needs be known to others. Holding everything inside may lead to letting others walk all over you or taking advantage of your good nature. You may have negative feelings about yourself or difficulties making decisions. Being too passive can cause worry about what others think about you or feelings of indifference to situations. It may seem as if you don't care when in fact you care very much. The Law of Passivity urges you to step out of your shell and become a more active participant in your life if you're too passive and to rein yourself in a bit if you're overly dominant.

Passive and Active Behavior

As you're making changes in your life to achieve the things you desire, take a good, hard look at yourself to see if you're demonstrating passive or active behavior. Do you often apologize for your feelings, edit your speech so you don't offend anyone, or put everyone else's needs before your own? Are you afraid to take risks because you always imagine the worst case scenario happening? Do you avoid making eye contact with others, belittle yourself or make excuses when someone is trying to place blame on you? Do you accept that blame even if it's not yours? Do you give others the authority to make decisions for you? Do you do things you really dislike simply because someone else wants you to do it? Do you always say yes when you want to say no? These are all characteristics of being too passive, which can lead to feeling that there isn't meaning to what you do or being overly critical of yourself.

If you're on the other end of the scale where you're an active participant in your life but you've become more dominating or rigid in your expectations, then you may find yourself telling others what to do all the time, expecting what you want when you want it without regard to the feelings of others, or becoming aggressive in nature when things don't happen exactly your way. You may have tunnel vision with only your needs and desires having any importance in your world. You may feel that you know everything and you're an expert on every subject. If someone is discussing something they've done, you've done it too but better than the other person could have ever done it. If these descriptions sound like you, then it's time for some deep reflection and change. Being too passive or too dominant causes negativity to block your path to success. If you take the time to reflect on your spiritual essence you can become centered within yourself so your actions are in balance.

Granted there are times when you need to take a passive stance just as there are times when you need to be an active decision maker in control of a situation. When you're able to balance the two, you can flow between both qualities with ease. The Law of Passivity warns against going to extremes in either case.

Words Can Change Passivity

To stop being too passive, change your words. Let's say you're in a lunch room and are looking for somewhere to sit. Instead of saying "Would you mind if I sit here?" ask instead, "Is this seat taken?" If the answer is no, have a seat and enjoy your lunch. If the answer is yes, then look for another seat using the same phrase. If you're having a conversation, say what you think instead of asking for the other person's permission by saying something like "if it's okay with you I would like to…" Now granted, there are times when you'll need to ask someone's permission before doing something but doing it continuously is passive behavior. Instead, you could say what you plan to do and ask if the person would like to join you. When you take control of your actions and words, and are confident in what you want to achieve, the results can be phenomenal. You become an active participant in your life which makes it easier to achieve all you desire. Be direct in your communication. Make statements that start with "I", be specific, and let your perspective be known. Be an active listener and come up with solutions to problems instead of taking blame for them onto yourself. Use your words to ensure that others aren't disregarding your opinions, wants, or needs. Taking these actions will help you move from being too passive to being more active—without becoming aggressive.

If you've realized you're too dominant, then you can change your words and how you approach people. Try to engage others in conversations where they feel important in the decision making process. When you include others and show them that their opinions have value, then you'll receive much more encouragement and cooperation from them as you try to achieve your goals. No one likes to feel as if they're being railroaded into doing something. When you listen to their thoughts and ideas, they're more willing to help you in your endeavors and you'll feel more inclined to help them in theirs.

Feelings of discomfort often accompany both passive and overly dominant behavior. Try to notice how you are reacting to others and how they are reacting to you. If you are feeling uncomfortable in a situation, instead of just going along with it, let your feelings be known. It will ease your discomfort, which the other person may not even be aware of until you tell them. If you notice someone isn't looking at you or they're simply agreeing with everything you say, that person is probably uncomfortable with you or the situation. Maybe they look up to you and want your approval and are afraid to say something wrong that might upset you or make you think less of them. If you feel this is what's happening, change the way the conversation or situation is going so that the person becomes more actively involved, leading to them feeling more comfortable.

The Law of Passivity means having a healthy respect for yourself and other people. When you're out of balance and too passive, you may not have enough self-respect or if you're too dominant you may have too little respect for others. It's when respect is lacking that success becomes difficult.

As you're reaching for your goals in life, remember that you are just as important as everyone else on the planet. Step up and reach for what you want, speak your mind, and know that it's completely okay to do so. If you've taken things too far then step back a bit and tone it down to make your path easier. We're all in this life together. Respect, help, and encourage one another to achieve greatness.

Try It Now

Passivity means stepping back from responding or taking action. Today, think about whether you should respond or act in situations you encounter or if this is a good time to be more passive and take a step back. Try to be more passive instead of active today. Notice the effects of passivity during your day.

Practical Application Tips

- If someone asks you for a favor or to do something for them, only say yes if you truly want to do it. There's nothing wrong with saying no. Just because someone asks something of you doesn't mean you have to do it.

- It's your right to change your mind, your opinion, and to take action accordingly.

- Avoid choosing the easy way out of a situation. Make the effort required to do things when they need to be done. Avoid being lazy.

- Don't be too hard on yourself. It takes time to change your ways.

- Release fear from your life. Stop worrying what other people think and do what you feel is right for your spiritual being.

- You are no one's doormat. Don't let other's take advantage of your good nature.

- Actively take control of your life in order to achieve the things you want to accomplish.

- Turn down the volume if you've become overly dominant in your pursuit of success.

- Respect yourself and those around you to achieve your desires. You will probably help another achieve their dreams as they help you achieve yours.

- Don't hold everything inside so it builds up. Eventually you'll explode or have a meltdown.

See Also Chapter 13: The Law of Action

24

THE LAW OF SACRIFICE

—🕊—

*Today I choose to let go of that which no longer
serves me in order to reach my greatest desire.*

THE LAW OF SACRIFICE states that in order to obtain something you want, you must lose, or let go of, something you currently have. This applies to every aspect of your life, from relationships to prosperity and affects the amount of time you have in a day. It's always a good idea to give first rather than lose unexpectedly later. Sacrifice means to give up something to achieve something else that has greater value to you. According to the American Heritage Dictionary, *sacrifice* is defined as "the act of offering something to a deity in propitiation or homage" and "the forfeiture of something highly valued for the sake of one considered to have a greater value or claim." In a religious context, it was the giving of items to the religion-specific gods to appease them. From a spirituality viewpoint, we think of it as voluntarily letting go of something to obtain something else you desire in order to appease yourself.

When you spend money on something you want, you're sacrificing the money for the item, but the item has greater value to you than the money does. If you want a car, you're willing to make monthly payments so that you'll have a vehicle that will get you where you need to go. If you desire a better paying job, you sacrifice the time and energy needed to move up the corporate ladder because you feel the increase in pay and a better job has more value than the time it takes to obtain it. The Law of Sacrifice can be very simple—you give this to get that—or it can be complex with unexpected consequences, especially if you ignore it. Think of a jar filled with marbles. Only so many marbles will fit inside the jar. When the jar is full to the brim, you must either take a marble out to put a new one in, or if you force it inside, another marble will pop out and it could be one you really wanted to keep. This is how the Law of Sacrifice works. You have a limited amount of space to hold everything you want. As you progress through life, you will change. Things you previously desired may no longer hold any appeal or be necessary. That's when you can willingly choose to let them go (take a marble out of the jar) or if you don't make the choice, the universe will do it for you (any marble can pop out when you put too many in the jar)!

I can't win for losing. Have you ever heard someone say that? It means they feel like they're always losing and never achieving anything good in their life. This happens when you only see what's leaving your life instead of what's coming into it.

The Law of Sacrifice can help you get unstuck from situations by forcing your hand or by putting you in a situation where the choice is taken from you. Maybe you'd been thinking about breaking up in your relationship but kept going back and forth on the issue. When the other party made the decision the choice was taken from you and you're left to deal with the loss. It may have been better to give that person their freedom on your own terms than to lose the ability to make the decision for yourself.

Finances and Sacrifice

Let's talk about money, the creation of wealth, and prosperity because it is something most people would like to achieve. Who wouldn't benefit from making more money? It can be hard to stay focused and positive if you're constantly worrying about money. If one of your goals is to increase your income, you must put in the effort required to gain more money. If you choose to go to school for a career that pays well, there will be times when you give up going out with friends or having a lazy day relaxing because you have to study. By choosing what you will sacrifice and giving those things up while you're preparing for your career, you're ensuring that when you land a successful position you haven't incurred any debt that will need to be repaid to the universe. When you see an overnight sensation who suddenly gains considerable success, take a moment to look at their career path. Has the actor who is starring in a movie had lots of bit roles prior to landing this part? If so, the actor has paid his dues and is now collecting a reward for the sacrifices made to achieve a starring role in a movie.

To move forward, you must also leave things behind. This is the Law of Sacrifice in action. When you try to hold onto things while moving forward, it simply doesn't work. You end up in a rut and never attaining what you desire. When you let go of the things you are willing to sacrifice so you may progress along your path, you resume forward motion. What if you achieve the six-figure income you so desperately wanted, and sacrificed your time and energy to attain it only to find out you'll have to move from one side of the country to another to work in your chosen field? You may resist because moving means leaving your friends and family behind, and you aren't going to see them much anymore, and talking on the phone isn't the same as being with them. If the job is something you've always dreamed of doing, you have to decide if the job is more important and has greater value to you or if being with your family and friends has greater value. Either way, you'll have to sacrifice one for the other. You can always call and visit your family and friends and take the job, or you can give up the job to stay close to home and hope that another position opens nearby. There are always choices to make when you're aware of and living the Law of Sacrifice.

Willingness to Sacrifice

If you want to achieve happiness in your life, have less frustration and regret, then understanding how the Law of Sacrifice works will help you. It's impossible to get what you want without being willing to give up something in return, but if you are unconditionally committed to and comfortable with the decisions and choices you make in life, then you will find happiness and have a great life without regret.

In life, you'll always find people who are willing to sacrifice more than others to achieve their dreams. The bigger your goals, the more sacrifices you'll make to get where you want to be. You'll meet people who talk about the great things they're going to achieve but then you see them never moving forward to actually achieve those goals. While these people may want to achieve things, they don't want to give up what they have in their lives now to get there. Not everyone will put in the same amount of effort to reach their goals. Those who do will succeed, those who don't will not. Only you can decide which type of person you are and how much you're willing to give up in order to get what you want. If you decide the sacrifices are worth the effort, then also know that you'll have to continue to give up things to maintain your success once you reach the place you want to be; otherwise, you run the risk of losing what you've worked so hard to achieve.

You have the dream and the desire. Make the sacrifices necessary to obtain all you want in life.

Try It Now

To see if you're willing to make the sacrifices necessary to obtain something you want, first look at others who have traveled similar paths. Don't look at only the end result; instead examine the work put into achieving that result. How many years does it take a musician or actor to achieve star status? What about a top-level business person or the entrepreneur who owns a multi-million-dollar company? Write down the things you would have to do in order to achieve your dream. Leave lots of space under each item because you're going to need it in a few minutes. After finishing the list write the things you would have to give up to reach the goal under each thing you'd have to do. Once you've finished your list, look at each one. Can you give up what you've written down to achieve what you want? Be honest with yourself. After you've evaluated what you'd like to achieve, you may find your original goal is not exactly right for you but you've come up with another goal which would be perfect for you during the evaluation.

Practical Application Tips

- Sacrifice something you feel has a lesser value in order to achieve something that has greater value to you.

- You are able, but you must also be willing. Where there is a will, there is a way.

- It's better to give up something first than to lose something you would rather have kept later.

- The Law of Sacrifice requires that all gains are paid for by a loss.

- When you resist sacrifices, you're blocking your forward movement toward your goals.

- You can't have what you want *and* what you have to give up. Make a choice.

- Be truthful with yourself. If you're not willing to give up something to get what you want then maybe you don't really want it.

- Once you get what you want, you'll have to keep giving to maintain it.

- If you're stuck, re-evaluate.

- Only you can decide if the sacrifices are worth the achievement.

See Also Chapter 33: The Law of Cycles

25

THE LAW OF
RESPONSIBILITY

*Today I take responsibility for myself, everyone, and
everything that I am charged with watching over.*

THE LAW OF RESPONSIBILITY states that as spiritual beings we are
to respond to the situations we find ourselves in and the people we encounter in an appropriate manner. Being responsible means we must
make our own decisions and act independently while being accountable for our actions without placing blame on others. Spiritually, we are
charged with a duty to handle our lives and those we are watching over
in a responsive and responsible way. Being morally responsible means
doing the right thing in difficult circumstances. It is our response to the
needs of others that enables us to grow, raise our frequency, and live the
Law of Responsibility.

When you're a responsible person, it means you look out for the welfare of others, for your own welfare, and for every situation you're charged with watching over. To be responsible for others, first be responsible for yourself. Take care of your emotional needs, your spirituality, and your physical body so you can meet the universe's challenges when you are required to be responsible for someone or something else.

Prove Your Responsibility to Gain More Abundance

To receive additional responsibility in life, you have to prove you can handle your current responsibilities. If you want to achieve financial success, learn to spend, save, and invest wisely. Once you do, you'll notice that more money flows to you because you've proven you can handle it. If you're always overdrawing your accounts or if you're constantly short on money to pay your bills because you spend it on things you wanted but didn't really need, then you'll find yourself in a position where you're always trying to make ends meet. Create a budget and then stick to it. You may have to choose to stay home when asked to go out with friends or decide against buying a new item you want, but budgeting will keep you on track and be beneficial in the long run. Not only will you have enough money each month for what you must pay because you're managing it better but you're also teaching yourself discipline.

The universe is always putting us in situations where we can prove we are responsible and make the right choices. It's up to us to choose the correct response and be responsible for our actions. Sometimes we may completely miss the opportunity to show how responsible we are, and if that happens, the universe will remove the opportunity and present it again sometime in the future. It's important to be aware and pay attention so when the opportunity arises you can take advantage of it. There will be times when you totally blow it and choose to be irresponsible, and the situation will be removed. In those cases, the opportunity will be presented again at a future date when hopefully you will respond appropriately, which shows you can now handle the responsibility.

Don't Blame Others for Your Actions

Being responsible for your actions means you're not putting the blame on someone else. It means if you're wrong, you admit you're wrong. Being responsible for others is all about how you care for them and how you treat them. When you blame others for your lack of responsibility, not only are you denying yourself the opportunity to move forward on your own spiritual path, but you're giving them power over you. They know they're not to blame, you know they're not to blame, so why blame them? Now they have something to hold over your head in the future if they want to act negatively toward you. By accepting blame anytime you're irresponsible then you retain your inner power, which makes you a stronger, more balanced person.

Spiritual and Emotional Growth

Spiritual growth is also based on responsibility. In life you will be presented with situations that test your spiritual beliefs. If you pass these tests, then you prove to the universe that you are handling your soul's growth and can handle even more. For instance, I did readings online for years before I ever charged for a reading. I used my intuition to help others. I never advertised my website and felt that if someone needed my help, they'd find me. As more and more people became aware of me, the time it took to do readings increased until I found that I didn't have the time I needed to do other things in my life. Then one day someone said it was okay to charge for readings because it gave them value. This made sense to me because as spiritual beings we all have a responsibility to place value on who we are and what we do. So I charged for readings, very little, but I put a price on my time. Over the years, as I received more rewards from the universe by showing my responsibility, those prices increased.

At this point, because I am teaching through writing books, I have had to put my readings on hold. This too is showing responsibility to myself and to those who want a reading with me. Eventually I plan to go back to doing readings, but right now I have a responsibility to write the best books I can, as it will help even more people than individual readings. As I grew spiritually, I had different opportunities present themselves where I could prove I was spiritually responsible for myself and others. Had I not proven myself in those cases, I would not have been presented with the opportunity to write books that could help thousands of people on a spiritual level. I am extremely grateful for the opportunity and hope you find benefit in my words.

The Law of Responsibility means you are also responsible for your own feelings. They are yours and yours alone. If you can't speak with someone about how you feel, without worrying about how they'll feel about your feelings, then you're taking responsibility for their emotions as well as your own. When you do this, you're giving yourself the burden of worrying about hurting their feelings when discussing your own and are projecting your feelings onto them. That's not really fair, is it? You're assuming they can't handle what you're feeling and that you must be untrue to your own feelings so you don't hurt them. You don't know how another person feels unless they tell you, and you could be completely misreading them. You may think someone is standoffish, when they're feeling surprised but just aren't expressing it to you.

Spiritually, it is not your responsibility to carry someone else's burden. They must carry it themselves in order to move forward along their spiritual path, just as you're moving forward along yours. When each of us carries our own burdens in life, when we take responsibility for our actions, our words, and everything we do, then we are deepening our spiritual connection to the whole. We are growing in responsibility and will be given more successes. Now, not taking on someone else's burden doesn't mean you can't give them a little help if needed. Words of guidance, confidence, or support let the other person know they have someone by their side, supporting them as they carry their burdens. You can help, you just can't take the burden from them and place it on your own shoulders. Doing so isn't fair to either party and will slow down the spiritual progress of both of you.

The Law of Responsibility can teach you valuable lessons; it can empower you and make you humble at the same time. It helps you realize life isn't just about the things happening to you on a daily basis; it is about how you respond to those things that counts. It can help you change on the inside, which will reflect changes in your reality. When you're responsible it is easy to achieve the things you want because not only are you giving yourself permission to receive them, you're saying you will take care of the things you receive because you have a responsibility to do so. When you prove you can handle more, the universe always gives you more.

Try It Now
Think of a recent situation where you didn't take responsibility for your actions. How did your actions affect other people? For example, maybe you didn't do your work at your job and someone else suffered the consequences because you slacked off. Take this opportunity to set things right with that person. You can apologize for your behavior, help them accomplish their tasks, or do something nice for them to make up for your actions. In the future, make sure you are always responsible for yourself and don't cause negativity for others because you've been irresponsible.

Practical Application Tips
- Take responsibility to experience spiritual growth, empowerment, and abundance.

- Being responsible means not taking on the burdens of others, which inhibits their own growth.

- Don't put blame on others for your lack of responsibility. Own up to your choices and decisions.

- If you act irresponsibly, that situation and responsibility will be taken from you and presented at another time. Be responsible to keep the opportunities given.

- When you prove responsibility, the universe will reward you with more things to be responsible for which results in more abundance in your life.

- When a situation seems out of control, analyze it to see if you need to accept responsibility in some way to bring it back into balance.

- Be responsible for yourself first so you can handle greater responsibilities successfully.

- Learn to let go of things you're trying to control that aren't your responsibility. Let the person who is responsible handle it.

- You are responsible for your soul's growth, so move forward in positivity and lightness of being.

- Accept responsibility in difficult situations to obtain balance, but only if the responsibility is yours to take.

See Also Chapter 9: The Law of Light

26

THE LAW OF ATTACHMENT AND DETACHMENT

—❧—

Today I will let go of attachments and obsessive behaviors. I will be fluid in my thoughts and creative in my approach to life. I will expect uncertainty and willingly accept all the universe has to offer.

THE LAW OF ATTACHMENT and Detachment states that you can have anything and everything you desire but when your happiness and sense of self-worth is dependent upon that thing then you are attached to it and must let it go, otherwise it controls you. In Taoism, Jainism, and Buddhism, detachment is a release from desire and consequently from suffering. This applies to material things, relationships, and any area of your life where you feel like you need something and can't live without it. Material things should be enjoyed as gifts received from universal abundance for your hard work. When you turn a gift into a need then you've put a condition on the gift and can become entangled in the web of angst you've surrounded it with.

Obsessing Over Things

It's one thing to desire a nice house or car, but if you turn obtaining them into an obsession then the effects can be negative. Instead of being comfortable within yourself and valuing yourself as a spiritual person, when your desire turns to an all-consuming need, it now affects all of the inner work you've done on yourself in a negative way too. What I mean by this is if you go from wanting a mansion in Beverly Hills to needing it to prove your worth, you've attached the house to your feelings of success. With this mentality, you'd consider yourself a failure if you weren't able to achieve that house. You don't have to prove you're worthy of the house to anyone, not even yourself, but if you think or feel you do, you're stuck in an attached mindset.

Let me give you an example. I'm attached to my horses because I love them deeply and even though we're breeders who raise and sell horses to others, I quickly become attached and form a bond with them and miss them terribly when they leave to go to their forever homes. That type of attachment is different then what the Law of Attachment and Detachment is talking about. The type of attachment this law is referencing is being so attached to something or someone that, if you don't have them or it in your life, you feel as if you have less value to yourself or others. If I sell a horse, even one I raised from birth, I will cry when they leave because I love them and I'll miss them but I don't feel any less of a person because they left. According to this law someone with an attachment to horses would feel their world just fell completely apart if they didn't have a horse in it and that their life no longer had meaning.

Being attached to things like houses, cars, animals, money, boats, or anything else you can own often leads to negative emotions like self-indulgence, jealousy, and arrogance. This type of attachment borders on obsession. It's important not to let your desire for something turn into an obsessive need attached to your self-worth.

Obsessing Over People

When you attach to people in the same way, guess what? Now they control you, they can manipulate you, and take advantage of you. Your obsessive attachment has given them power over your thoughts, actions, and the choices you make because you've given them more power and control over your being than you're keeping for yourself. If you find yourself in a situation like this, ask yourself why you feel this way. Why are you obsessing over this person? Why are you giving away your power? Why do you feel you'll be less than the wonderfully fantastic spiritual being you are if this person wasn't in your life? Is it because you're afraid of being alone? Is it because losing them would mean you'd have to find someone else? It is important to your spiritual growth to never base how you feel about yourself on whether or not another person is part of your life. One of the most important lessons is to stand on our own two feet, by ourselves, and face who we are at a soul level and take responsibility for what we're doing on the physical plane. Each of us deserves love and respect and a relationship with someone with whom we're on equal footing. Obsessive attachment doesn't have a place in a successful relationship because it makes it out of balance. It can make it difficult to leave relationships that are no longer in your best interest because you're always making excuses for the person you're attached to for their behavior. To create a lasting, loving relationship with someone, it must be based on unconditional love and complete acceptance of the other person, faults and all.

If you're obsessively attached to someone else, have you stopped to think how your attachment makes them feel? Some people may take complete advantage of you because when you're obsessively attached, you're vulnerable to them. Other people may feel very uncomfortable with your overt interest in them and may try to steer you away because they feel you're being clingy, needy, and are smothering them with your attention, which may also be unwanted. Their pushing you away is actually for your own good and spiritual growth … but only if they can get that message through to you, which can be difficult to do with someone who is obsessive in their attachment. The real issue with relationship attachments is that we all want to be seen, heard, and appreciated for our uniqueness and individuality. We all want to be loved. When we put all our energy on obtaining these things from the outside, from other people, before we learn to love and appreciate the unique beings we are, then we're not really giving ourselves unconditional love. Until we can unconditionally love ourselves, we can't truly love another or move forward on our spiritual path.

Attachment is usually based on fear and causes rigid thinking and expectations because you believe you need something or someone other than yourself to be happy. When you expect happiness to come from the outside instead of from your inner self, then other people will disappoint you when they no longer make you happy. But that's not on them; it's on you for being overly attached with unrealistic expectations. Everyone wants to be recognized as the unique, special person they are inside but your light can't shine as brightly when you dim it through attachments. When you release this fear, and realize you don't need anyone or anything else to make you happy, then you're practicing the detachment part of the Law of Attachment and Detachment.

When you let go of any attachments you've formed its easier for the universe to respond and provide you with the abundance you deserve and would like to receive. You can be focused on your goal with an intense passion without being obsessive and attached to it. If you feel as if you're crossing the line into obsessive attachment, then pull yourself back. Ask yourself if you're becoming too fixated in achieving the goal. If you are, make changes. There's nothing wrong with being intense in your actions but it is negative to be obsessive in them.

What really happens when you detach from attachments? You develop an understanding of your inner self, are compassionate toward yourself, and are able to understand the other person's point of view or realize why you don't need that thing in your life to be happy. Attachments can't be sustained. They always eventually break down or fall apart, and if you're not comfortable with your inner self, you'll have a difficult time. It's better yet to let go of all attachments and to stand as a detached observer for a while to gain a fuller understanding of yourself and those around you.

Detaching from attachments can be a little scary because you're moving from a place of obsession to uncertainty, from trying to control to letting go of control, but when you're willing to make this change, to detach, you release yourself from past conditioning and obstacles that prevent you from connecting to your true spiritual self. Let go to fly free.

Try It Now

When you let go of attachments you are progressing along your spiritual path. Today take a walk where you can watch people. Do you see any obsessive tendencies or interactions between people? Maybe one person is acting jealous because their partner glanced at someone else that was nice looking. Or another couple is having an argument because one person is trying to control the actions or speech of the other. Now think of your situation. Have you been controlling or jealous? Are any of the behaviors you noticed among others also happening in your life? Sometimes it's hard to see what we're doing to ourselves, that's why I want you to observe others. As a quiet observer, we often see what we overlook in ourselves. If you discover that you're exhibiting symptoms of attachment, decide what you can do to change yourself and release it. It may take a little time but you can do it.

Practical Application Tips

- Let go of that which no longer serves you.

- The universe can't respond if you're blocking it with your attachments. Let them go to receive.

- Your self-worth should never be based on someone else's opinion or obtaining an object.

- Detaching from attachments can make you feel uncertain about the future. Look at it as an adventure and a new page in your life that's filled with freedom.

- If you feel obsessively attached to someone else, look at the situation from their point of view to get a clearer picture of your actions.

- Attachment is based on fear. Detachment is based on unconditional love for yourself.

- Attachments never last because of the inappropriate need associated with it.

- Disappointments come from attachments.

- Having attachments means you're giving away your power. Detach to become true to your spiritual self.

- To achieve success, release attachments, and move forward with passion.

See Also Chapter 38: The Law of Balance and Polarity

27
THE LAW OF FAITH

Today I have faith that my world is as it should be,
I will overcome any obstacles that I encounter
as I work toward achieving my goals.

THE LAW OF FAITH states that if you believe in something with strong conviction and trust that what you believe in will happen, then it will and the impossible will become reality. The Law of Faith is our direct connection to universal wisdom. With faith, there is no room for doubt. Be committed to your belief and trust in the Divine to bring about what you believe in. When you have faith, you lack fear. This is because you're listening to your inner guidance and know without a doubt you will receive the outcome you desire because you have faith in it. The Law of Faith is mentioned in the King James version of the Bible, in Romans 3:27: "Where is boasting then? It is excluded. By what law? Of works? Nay: but by the law of faith."

The Law of Faith is not connected to any religion; anyone can be filled with faith. The Law of Faith means believing when there is no proof that what you believe in will come about. It requires complete confidence, trust, and an unwavering belief. It means blocking out naysayers who will try to put doubt in your mind. Instead, listen to your intuitive inner self for guidance and to strengthen your faith. The power of faith is one of the strongest emotions. Faith is unwavering, committed, and fearless.

Faith is the belief in the Divine, of universal abundance, and in God, the Creator, the Source. Faith means knowing everything will work out as Divinely planned if it is for the greater good of all. Faith goes beyond the things you have learned about spirituality. It is an emotion of the highest frequency possible. There will be times when things you want don't manifest when you want them, but if you hold onto your faith, you will receive what you desire when the time is right. Other times, things may not happen at all because they're not for the greater good of all. For example, say you have faith that something you want will happen, but that something could emotionally hurt the person you're in a relationship with. Then the thing you believe will happen may not happen because it's not for the greater good of all involved. Fast-forward a few years: you're no longer in the relationship but you still have faith that what you wanted in the past will happen. At this point in time it can happen because there's no one who will be negatively affected by you receiving what you want. You never gave up faith, and though the time wasn't right before, it is now. That's why you can't put time limits on what you want to achieve in life. Everything happens in its own time.

Don't confuse the power of faith with what is called blind faith. If you have blind faith it means you're simply hoping something will happen when you haven't worked to achieve it or built the foundation on which it will grow. This often happens when you don't see the oneness of the Divine but instead see what you want as separate from the universal whole. Faith can create miracles; blind faith can create problems.

If you're practicing blind faith, your odds of achieving what you want will not be as successful. It's hit or miss. Sometimes things will happen as you want them to but more often they don't because you don't have the purity and power of real faith working for you.

Faith in Your Intuition

In today's world, everyone wants proof of how things work. Sometimes you must have faith in what you cannot see and what cannot be proven. You will most certainly face some kinds of adversity because of your faith. It doesn't matter what the belief, there are always people in the world who want to put your faith to the test because they can't prove its existence. A perfect example of this is intuition. You can't prove your hunches, impressions, or intuition. They just happen. A medium can't prove that the Spirit they see or hear is there, all they can do is deliver the message and hope it strikes a chord in the person who receives it. When no one else sees what you see, then there is nothing left but belief and faith that the impression is correct and will be meaningful to the person who is receiving the message.

When it comes to intuition, the reason everyone wants proof is because no intuitive is 100 percent accurate. If they say they are, find another intuitive for your reading. We can't be 100 percent accurate, because then there would be no reason to be on the earthly plane learning lessons. If you could see all, you would be God. There has to be room for error in order for the intuitive person to learn, which makes doubt in intuition easy for those who don't believe in intuition or psychic abilities. Here's an example. I've done intuitive readings for a very long time. It is an integral part of who I am. I have absolute faith that what I sense, what I see, is what the person needs to know at the time of the reading. It might not always make sense to them at that moment, but in the future it will. I remember once when I'd first started doing readings for the public online and I had a large influx of people wanting readings in a short span of time. I did the readings and people gave me feedback about my accuracy level. Their comments were stunning because I'd been unbelievably accurate in what I'd said to them. Ego got in the way, and I started thinking about how great I was for being so accurate all the time. And sure enough, the universe took my ego right back down to size—every reading I did for two weeks afterward was completely wrong until I realized that I'd gotten too big for my britches in my thinking. Once I learned my lesson and put ego aside, my readings were accurate again, and my belief and faith in myself and universal guidance was restored. Ego has a way of messing up the path you're walking by making you believe too much in your greatness and having less faith in what the universe has in store for you.

Faith Leads to Enlightenment

The more faith you have the more enlightened you become. You'll see things clearly as they are instead of through rose-tinted glasses. Faith doesn't apply only to a specific religion. Many different religions, and those who don't practice a specific religion, all believe in the power of faith because it is a universal law, an enormously high frequency, which is part of our connection to the oneness of the universe. It is part of us all and as such it is important that we have faith in our lives. When you have faith, anything and everything is achievable. Your success is limited only by the power of your faith in your success. As spiritual beings, faith is crucial to our existence. When you understand you're connected to the oneness of the whole and have faith that what you're trying to achieve will come to fruition, the universe delivers what your faith perceives.

Faith works: it heals and is a driving force within us. It doesn't matter if what you desire is big or small, or if a situation or problem is simple or complex. All that matters is you have faith that you will receive a solution to the problem or obtain what you desire. Faith gives you a reason to keep going when you may want to give up. It can help you overcome temporary setbacks along your path.

Try It Now

How do you recognize faith? It is believing. It is a feeling deep within you that no one else experiences in the same way you do. To recognize what faith feels like to you, find a quiet place where you can retreat within to connect with your spiritual being. Ask your higher self to wrap your faith around you like a blanket. Visually imagine what it feels like. Is it soft, strong, filled with power? Does it vibrate in tune with your own vibration or is it a deep thumping sound. Let yourself visualize how your faith presents itself to your inner essence. Then whenever you feel your faith slipping as negativity tries to work its way inside you, pull out your blanket of faith and wrap it around you, letting it empower and strengthen your faith.

Practical Application Tips

- Faith is not associated with any specific religion. Anyone can have faith because it is the connection to universal wisdom and the Divine.

- Faith fills you with strong convictions and trust that things will work out for the greater good of all. If something isn't working out the way you want, the time isn't right.

- Faith eliminates fear, which can hold you back from reaching goals.

- Faith can't be proven but it is stronger than any other emotion and has a very high frequency. To raise your own frequency, have faith.

- Be wary of blind faith. It can give you false hope and lead to problems.

- To practice faith, know what you want, believe you will attain it, then let it go, having faith you will achieve it or it will be given to you when the time is right. Letting go and releasing control is a key element in faith.

- If you don't achieve something as quickly as you desire, remember that the universe works on its own time table. Have faith you will achieve what you want in time.

- Leave doubt behind and allow faith to fill the void.

- Never give up your faith. It will carry you through any difficulties along your path, making them easier to overcome. As a spiritual being, faith is crucial to our existence.

See Also Chapter 11: The Law of Purpose

28

THE LAW OF ATTENTION

— 🕊 —

*I am fully aware of where my attention is
focused and will keep it positive and in forward
motion to bring myself happiness and joy.*

THE LAW OF ATTENTION states that anything you put your attention on will manifest in your life. This is a simple law but is very important in achieving success and obtaining the things you want. When you give something your attention, especially your undivided focus, its energy grows and expands as it is drawn to you.

What is attention? It is the ability to concentrate, to keep your mind on task, to focus. It is what you think about, the use of your words, and the actions you take based on those thoughts and words. The amount of time you spend thinking and talking about something also adds to the focus you're giving it. The more time and energy given to something, the more likely you'll achieve it. In *Meditations of the First Philosophy* by Rene Descartes, published in 1625, the author states that everything can be doubted. When objections to this concept arose, Descartes responded by stating that it is only when we pay attention that clear ideas provides a place where doubt does not take hold.

If you find your thoughts turning toward the negative then turn those thoughts into positive ones to regain your focus and get your attention back on the matter at hand. We all have different expectations from ourselves when trying to attain goals because we have different ideas about what the outcome of reaching that goal will be. Some people may push themselves to the extreme, take on too many tasks, and thrive on the excitement and hard work of doing a lot of things at once. Others need to take it slower, not have too much on their plate at one time, and while they still work hard, it's at a different pace. Some people may work on the goal for a while then take a long break before coming back to it. There is less urgency in reaching an end result. We each create our own reality based on our unique connection to the Divine and the energy we put into giving our attention to reaching our goals. What is right for someone else may not be right for you. There may be other things pulling your attention away from a much desired goal but the other thing may really need more of your attention at that moment in time. That's life. That's how things work. Even if you have to pull your attention away from something for a while, it's okay. You can always go back to it later. The main thing is that you never give up on your dreams and always keep giving them your attention in your mind even if you can't actively give more of your attention to the work needed to reach the end result.

Self-Fulfilling Prophecies

I'm sure you've probably heard the saying, *be careful what you wish for because you just might get it*. Be careful with your thoughts and words. Keep them powerful, positive, and filled with light. Work through any feelings of fear or negativity instead of ignoring or repressing them. That way they don't dominate your thoughts as worst case scenarios When you are always afraid of what might happen, then you're drawing those things to you according to the Law of Attention. You're giving those negative things power over you by thinking about them, talking about them, and letting them fester inside of you when there's no reason to let that happen. Fill your mind with positive attention on the things you want to happen instead of negative attention about what could happen in a worst-case scenario. Hold a vision of what you want in your mind, give it your full attention and ask it to come to you.

Self-fulfilling prophecies can be created by giving what you want your focused attention. They can also be created by giving what you fear too much attention. Which would you rather have? Most people prefer the self-fulfilling prophecy that gives them what they want in life instead of what they fear. So why put your energy and attention on something you fear? That's just defeating your own purpose isn't it? When you think of giving something your attention in this manner it helps you to see clearly how to manifest what you want. You don't want to achieve something that you wouldn't want to happen, so why would you give those possibilities your attention? Don't. There's no reason for you to have a negative experience in life because you're letting fear and worry get inside you and mess up your positive thoughts.

As spiritual beings, our ability to focus our attention on something and then gain that something because our energy draws it to us, is a gift from the universe. If we're unaware of the true nature of this gift, and how we can use it to get ahead in life on the physical plane, and to understand the principles of the spiritual plane so we can connect to the Divine, then we are doing ourselves a disservice. Within our frequency, at the core essence of our beings, we know all of the spiritual laws of the universe. We understand how they work and what we should do to make our lives in the physical realm successful so we learn the lessons necessary to grow spiritually. It is our job, right now in this moment, to remember this information, especially how to use the Law of Attention. As we seek out information from the Divine and search for answers to our individual existence, our purpose, and how we can become more connected to our true spiritual essence, it is mandatory that we conduct this search with our eyes wide open and our attention focused on inner truth.

We always have complete control over our attention. It is mandatory for our survival. Wild animals must keep their attention on their environment at all times in order to remain safe from predators and live. If they let their attention slack, they become prey. It's the same with humans. Look at how many people have hurt themselves because they put their attention on their cell phones instead of paying attention to where they are walking. When you put your attention onto something so much that you're no longer paying attention to your safety, and you notice this happens repeatedly, then it's time to evaluate what you're doing. If the phone is causing you that much distraction and taking your attention away from your job or your family, you may find yourself out of a job and in arguments with family, but you'll probably be doing great with friends because you're texting them and ignoring everyone and everything else you're responsible for interacting with on a daily basis.

When we put our attention on developing our spirituality and our connection to the Divine, we are fulfilling part of our purpose on the earthly plane. Spiritual transformation can be brought about by nurturing our attention to our spirituality, letting it become such an integral part of our beings that even when our attention is elsewhere, there is still a large degree of our attention subconsciously focused on the Divine. When this happens, you awaken on a spiritual level. You become aware that you are part of the universal consciousness, part of the whole. Once awakened, you'll have passed into a more aware state of mind where you understand the importance of putting your attention on the things in life that will enhance your being, ensure your success, and transform you spiritually.

Where you place your attention can make or break you. It is powerful and strong. Become aware of the things and people to whom you're giving your attention. If you are putting your attention on the wrong things, now is the time to make a change and redirect your attention back to the priorities in your life.

Try It Now

You may not even be aware that you're giving negativity your attention. To see if you are or not, call up a close friend and have a conversation. Don't tell them that you're doing it but make sure you pay attention to what you're saying and if something you say comes across as negative, jot down a little note about it or even record your side of the conversation. After you hang up the phone, look at what you've written down or play back the recording of yourself. How could you have said things differently so they came across positive instead of negative? Do you notice a pattern? Is there something worrying you subconsciously that came across in the conversation that you didn't even realize was bothering you? This is a good way to get a handle on how you're speaking and what you're giving your attention during a conversation. The more aware you are, the easier it will be to notice when you're putting your attention in the wrong place. Once you're aware, then you can correct the behavior.

Practical Application Tips

- You do not have unlimited attention. When you put your attention on something you're diverting it from something else.

- Everything you do requires some degree of your attention.

- Become aware of where you're placing your attention in order to use the Law of Attention to your benefit.

- Whatever you give your attention to, will come to you.

- Refrain from giving negativity your attention.

- Create self-fulfilling prophecies by putting your attention on the positive things you want to happen in your life.

- Being unaware isn't an excuse for not paying attention to what you want to achieve in life. Only you can create your own reality and success by paying attention to what you want to achieve.

- You have complete control over what you give your attention to. Do so wisely.

- When in doubt, don't. Doubt will put your attention on the negative, which will have the opposite result of what you're trying to achieve. Believe in yourself and put your attention on your success.

- Awaken spirituality by putting your attention on your connection to the Divine.

See Also Chapter 6: The Law of Intention

29

THE LAW OF FORGIVENESS

— 🕊 —

*I release negativity by forgiving those who have
hurt, offended, or upset me and send them love.*

THE LAW OF FORGIVENESS is based in love and refers to releasing
anger, resentment, hatred, bitterness, or other negative emotions toward someone or something; to pardon them for any wrongs done to
you, whether known or unknown to them. Forgiveness is a key component in many religions, including Judaism, Buddhism, and Christianity to name a few. Forgiveness is also an important part of relationships
and human interactions.

Every person can choose to live by the Law of Forgiveness. When
you forgive someone, you're allowing love to overcome negative feelings thereby releasing any animosity you have toward the other person.
Forgiveness isn't about accepting someone's bad behavior or excusing

it away or saying their actions were right. It's about letting go of any negative feelings within yourself caused by their actions so they don't have a negative long-term effect on you and no new karma is created. It doesn't matter if the wrong done to you was done purposefully or was an honest mistake if your feelings are hurt. You're releasing your feelings when you forgive someone, which in turn will affect their feelings. Some people will be relieved you're no longer angry or upset with them. Others will care less what you think or feel because they don't care if you forgive them or not. The faster you can break any type of connection with them through forgiveness the better.

I know this is easier said than done. Forgiving someone isn't always an easy choice to make, especially if they've hurt you. Forgiveness can take you through some very complex emotions that help you heal yourself so you're able to forgive without repressing anything regarding the situation or falling into self-judgment. But once you reach that point and you've worked through the emotions for yourself, you'll be able to forgive. You will have grown spiritually and the negativity will no longer be part of you.

Steps to Forgiveness

When you forgive, you're letting go of future karma. You're acknowledging that the situation affected you and you're forgiving the actions of the other person so this particular lesson won't be repeated in your future lives. That doesn't mean there isn't some kind of karmic debt to be repaid on the part of the other person unless they forgive themselves for their actions too. As spiritual beings we are all part of the whole, we are all one. So when you forgive another person, aren't you really forgiving yourself too?

There are several steps involved in the process of forgiving someone who has hurt you. Forgiving someone isn't for them, it's for you so that you can let go of negative emotions surrounding the experience and move on with your life. Address your feelings by identifying who hurt you and how you felt about the experience. You may feel anger, hatred, disappointment, and other similar emotions as you go back to the source of the event. In order to forgive, these emotions must be faced and worked through. Be sure to include why the actions are not okay for you. Understand that withholding forgiveness is only hiding your pain away and repressing it. Until you face it, the pain will always be held within you. It takes time to heal as you work through the process of forgiveness. Instead of replaying the experience over and over in your mind and experiencing the pain of the hurt repeatedly, think of a positive goal you can achieve based on the experience and work towards that goal. When you forgive and move on with your life, you remove the power that the person who hurt you has over you. When you focus on feeling more joy and happiness in your life, you can move the event into the past. Most importantly, always make an agreement with yourself to do whatever is required so that you can feel better and move forward. You should always be kind to yourself because forgiving someone is difficult work. It's going to take you time and space to get to the point where you can say that you truly forgive the person.

Forgiveness Heals

Forgiveness is a high frequency emotion. It empowers, heals, and releases karma for the person doing the forgiving, if you really mean it. If you haven't forgiven the person in your heart and let go of all negative emotions associated with the situation and their actions, then you really haven't forgiven them, regardless of how many times you say you have. Forgiveness has to be complete. Any little niggling piece of animosity will fester into a boil if it's not completely released when you forgive. Forgiving someone also means looking at and taking responsibility for your part in the situation too. Have you done something you need to apologize for in addition to forgiving the other person? Do they need to forgive you as well? When you forgive yourself for your part of the situation, let the love you have for yourself replace any negative feelings you may be holding about your part in the event and forgive yourself.

Have you ever told someone you've forgiven them but you'll never forget what they've done? That's not true forgiveness. If you're going to always remember the transgression, then it's still a part of you, eating away at you at some hidden level. When you forgive, you also have to forget.

When negative feelings about someone else build up inside of you because you haven't yet forgiven them, it causes you harm. You may be upset all the time, easily frustrated, or you might even make yourself sick or depressed. To regain your positive state of mind, forgive them and yourself while releasing the emotions associated with the situation or person. If you're not sure if you've been successful at forgiveness, just take a moment to think of a past situation where someone did you wrong. How do you feel after remembering the event? Did you tense up or get mad or frustrated at them all over again simply by thinking about the situation? If you did, you haven't really forgiven them. If you think about the situation and don't feel anything negative but see it as something that happened to you that you've moved past, then you have really given your forgiveness to the other person involved, the situation itself, and yourself.

Forgiveness as Transformation

Forgiveness is an integral part of spiritual transformation. Your spiritual energy can't move into higher frequencies if you're holding onto anger towards someone you should forgive. But once you've forgiven, those emotions are released and your spiritual self can move forward. Imagine your spiritual self trying to push through a fence of ropes. The ropes have some give to them when you press forward, but they put pressure on your energy and no matter how hard you try, you can't push through. But when you identify the situation the rope represents and forgive, the rope snaps, giving you more freedom and helping your inner self to heal. When all the reasons have been identified, every rope will have snapped, allowing you to continue your soul growth. If you can't see what's holding you back, try meditating about it, using creative visualization during your meditation to discover what the ropes represent. You may be surprised to find something you thought was long past is still holding you back.

Practicing forgiveness brings change. It can help mend relationships, heal broken hearts, and put you back on the path you're traveling if you've wandered off that path. Forgiveness is powerful, it is of the light, and necessary for life to flow with peace and harmony. When you're called on to offer forgiveness to another, you're not only forgiving them, but you're forgiving yourself, releasing any power they held over you when you lacked forgiveness. Being able to forgive enables you to reach higher frequencies and gain spiritual empowerment.

Try It Now

Let's talk about forgiving yourself for a moment. It's really difficult to forgive yourself, isn't it? When that little chatterbox gets going in your mind, replaying what you could have done differently (especially if you were in the wrong), it's not easy to quiet it down. Your higher self is in there too, trying to help you forgive yourself but that chatterbox can talk a mile a minute and be very loud, sometimes talking right over your higher self in an effort to take all your attention and tell you all of the negative aspects of what happened and how you could have behaved differently. When you realize this is happening, stop whatever you're doing and focus inside your mind on getting the chatterbox to quiet down. I often say *shhhhh* or *hush* in my mind and then try very hard to hear what my higher self is saying. When you stop giving the chatterbox your attention, you will be able to hear your higher self clearly. So when the chatterbox is having a field day in your mind, divert your attention and let go of the negativity keeping you from loving yourself enough to forgive yourself for whatever needs to be forgiven.

Practical Application Tips

- Forgiveness allows you to let go of emotions that are holding you back from reaching your desires.

- To be successful, practice forgiveness.

- Spiritual transformation requires that you forgive others, situations, and yourself.

- A lack of forgiveness can cause you emotional and physical stress, even illness.

- Make it a habit every day to instantly forgive others. Sometimes it's easy if the problem is small, but other problems may take more time and energy on your part to truly forgive.

- If you offer forgiveness, mean it. If you don't mean it yet, don't say it.

- Quiet the chatter in your mind to find the love of your higher self which will help you forgive.

- Forgiveness means honoring your own path and the path of others.

- Forgiveness helps you heal if you give it freely and without conditions.

- Be open and allow the time it takes to arrive at forgiveness.

See Also Chapter 10: The Law of Unity

30

THE LAW OF REQUEST

— 🕊 —

*Today I am open to asking for assistance with love
and positivity and accepting help when I need it.*

THE LAW OF REQUEST states that if you need help you must ask for it,
be ready to receive it, and you should not offer help unless it is requested
by another. It originates in the early Christian religion in the Bible books
of Matthew and James. Unrequested help doesn't apply to random acts of
kindness. It specifically means not interfering in someone else's problems
because you have an issue with their problem and think you can solve it
better than they can. The Law of Request is about what the universe can
do for you, not what you can do for another person.

Because we all have free will, the universe and the beings that live in
the spiritual realm don't just pop in and interfere with the lessons we're
learning on the earthly plane. While there are miraculous interventions

that do occur, this is a random act of kindness, preventing something that's not written in our charts from happening, and isn't considered interference.

We have to ask for universal help when it is needed in order to receive it. Once we ask, assistance is freely given. Be sincere in your request: ask for what you need from a place of love and show gratitude for the help. Try not to be demanding nor assume you are entitled to get everything you want. There are times when you may ask for something but it's not something you'd planned to receive before incarnating, or it may be something that if given, will interfere in your ability to learn the lessons you need to learn.

Signs in Unexpected Places

The help we receive doesn't always come in the form of a direct answer or immediate action. I often tell people if they're pondering a problem to ask their guides for assistance and then look for signs that point to the answer. There have been many, many times when I needed guidance and ended up in a bookstore. I would ask my guides to direct me to the book that would help me in my current situation. Then I would wander around, going up and down all the aisles until I felt drawn to a book. Often, it was a book that had nothing to do with the situation and it wouldn't be self-help. The energy of the book would speak to me on a soul level, and once I picked it up and opened it, some part of the text would look like it was raised higher than the rest. Whatever the text was, it was always meaningful to my situation. So my guides answered my call for help by directing me to the text that would strike a chord within me regarding my problem. I am always thankful for the assistance.

The Law of Request also relates to everything outside of the spiritual realm as well. If you need help, other people can't read your mind. They don't know what is going on inside you and can't help you unless you ask them to. Sometimes it means you have to open up and let them in before they can offer assistance. Fear of appearing weak or needy may hold you back but if you really, truly need help, let others offer a hand, shoulder, or the love that goes along with helping someone else in a difficult situation.

I worked in retail management for many years. Each and every time that I found myself looking for a new job, if it was a job that I felt would be a good fit for me and one I really wanted, I always asked the interviewer for the job. Sometimes it was a formal request if the interviewer was stern and if they were more laid back I'd say something like, "I'd like to work for your company. When can I start?" There were times when the interviewer would be surprised in their response to which I'd reply something along the lines of, "If I don't tell you how much I want this job and ask you to give me a chance, then how will you know?" Other times the interviewer would tell me I had *gumption* and hire me on the spot. When you are going after things you want in life you often have to request them from other people. I wanted the job so I asked for the job. This is the Law of Request in action. The next time you need help or want something that will lead you toward your goal, ask for it with positivity.

Challenges on the Earthly Plane

Living on the earthly plane has many unique challenges. One of those challenges is when you want to jump in and help someone when they're in a difficult situation without being asked. Of course you mean well, but sometimes meaning well can turn someone else's situation into a bigger problem. Just like the universe doesn't interfere with our learning experiences it's not our place to interfere in another person's earthly experience unless they specifically and directly ask for our help. That's so hard to do isn't it? Especially if they're making decisions you know will be a mistake based on your own life experiences. But it's their path. If they ask, you can advise. But if they don't ask and you interfere with what you feel they should do about the situation, then not only are you hampering your own soul growth, you're hampering theirs as well. They may feel like they're being put in the middle between you and the person they're involved with (if it's a relationship issue), and that makes life harder for them. How can they decide what steps to take if you're constantly trying to influence them with what you would or would not do if you were in their shoes? It can get very aggravating. If you think you might be doing this, stop and think about your actions. Are you trying to manage the situation because you were in a similar one where you were too controlling and got so emotionally hurt that you never got over it? That was a lesson for you, but it may not be the lesson for them. Maybe the lesson for them is to learn compromise where your lesson was to be less controlling. We all have different lessons, and inserting ourselves and our opinions into someone else's lesson may just backfire on you, distancing you from the person you want to help. When they are ready to receive your help and want your advice, they'll ask for it.

There are times when the answers you need are already within you. By looking within, you can often find those answers. If you're in a job that makes you unhappy but it is a necessary step to achieve your ultimate goal of a specific career, then maybe that's not the right career for you and you need to change your path. Or, it may be that you need to learn a life lesson through the experience of the job you dislike in order to appreciate your dream job when you get to it. Maybe you want to own a restaurant but to get the whole restaurant experience, you must work bussing tables and washing dishes, which you really dislike. But it's part of what you need to know about restaurant operations to be a successful owner. You may have to jump into any job within the restaurant at any given time without notice, so you need the knowledge beforehand. You also gain insight from the dishwasher's point of view and might even make changes that will help the restaurant run better because of the experience. It's a stepping stone on your way to your ultimate goal or could be a game changer based on your experience.

Asking for help can be hard to do especially if you are someone who doesn't want to feel like they owe someone something because they helped you. When assistance is given from the heart, you're not going to feel like that, and you never know what wonderful things you will experience or the knowledge you will gain simply by asking for help with grace and love.

Try It Now

How can you make reaching a goal easier if you ask for help from someone? What will it cost you to ask for help? Will it hurt your pride, cause you embarrassment, or make you feel less about yourself because you needed help? We all need help at some point in our lives and we all give help when asked at some point. If you feel the cost is worth the assistance, then ask someone to guide you. Or, if you really want something in life, ask someone in a position to help you achieve it, to give it to you or open doors for you that will lead to the goal. If you're having trouble deciding, write it down, work it out within yourself, and if you can't find the answer inside, ask someone to help you. It's not going to be the end of the world if you get help and you just might learn something new that you will carry with you for the rest of your life.

Practical Application Tips

- Asking for help doesn't mean you're weak. It means you're strong and realize when you need assistance.

- Don't try to overtake someone else's situation. They have to learn just like you do.

- When asked for help, give it with love in your heart, without being judgmental, and with sincerity.

- Every decision is an opportunity to learn. Don't deny someone else the chance to grow spiritually by interfering.

- Many of the answers you seek are already within you.

- If you are to receive, you must first ask.

- Be clear and specific in your request for help.

- Making decisions for someone else causes resentment and can damage relationships. Always allow others to make their own decisions even if you don't agree with them.

- Be ready to receive help when you request it. If you're not ready, don't ask.

- Respect the Divine in every person.

See Also Chapter 14: The Law of Affirmation

31
THE LAW OF ALLOWING

I will allow all that I desire to come to me. I will mind my own business and let universal energy do its job.

THE LAW OF ALLOWING states that you must trust in and allow the natural flow of life without resistance and with acceptance. Universal energy flows in currents, like a river flows within its banks. This concept originates from the beginnings of many religions because belief and acceptance go hand in hand with allowing. When followers believe, they are in line with the flow of life according to those beliefs, which allows for acceptance instead of resistance to life experiences. The Law of Allowing means the situations and people you encounter must be accepted as they are so they can move freely within the ebb and flow of these currents. From this natural flow comes growth. The Law of Allowing means to allow others to follow their own current and flow, even if what they're doing goes against what we believe or even if we feel they are making mistakes. It's their path; they must walk it to learn their own lessons.

The Law of Allowing means you don't know the best possible outcome to any given situation, even if you think you've got it all figured out. You are on the earthly plane of existence so you can't be aware of the karma involved with another person's life, the life map they charted prior to birth, or the lessons they're supposed to learn. We hardly know these things for ourselves so how can we know them for another person? There's just no way for us to have all the information needed to determine the best outcome, however, the universe knows and often the outcome we imagined will be far surpassed by the wonderful things actually delivered. It's a great mystery of the universe until it arrives in your life. This is where the Law of Allowing comes into place. As adults, we must allow things to flow freely towards us, allow others to do what they want, when they want, and for the reasons they want, and all without our interference. This doesn't apply to children who are still in need of an adult's protection and guidance.

Letting Go of Control by Being Open

When it comes to your own life, you have to let go of control, allow situations to unfold as they're meant to so the universe can create what you desire and manifest it freely within your life. If you allow the universe to work with your energy to create the things you desire without interference from you, then life flows smoothly and is less stressful while you're reaching your goals. When you try to control instead of allowing, you're placing blocks in your path.

To live by the Law of Allowing, you must be open and accepting to every situation you experience. Trust that what is being given to you is coming from universal abundance, that it is in your best interest, and there is much more out there for you if you believe in the unlimited abundance of the universe and allow it to enter your life.

Understanding the flow associated with the Law of Allowing will help you eliminate fear and negativity. You may have a subconscious fear of being successful, or of being alone or taken for granted. Whatever the fear, it will hold you back. If you find yourself in opposition instead of allowing, then it's time to find out *why* you're resisting and if you have an unresolved fear.

There are feelings of relief, acceptance, and freedom in allowing things to happen as they happen, allowing people to be who they are, and allowing yourself to experience acceptance. Have you ever heard the saying *it is what it is*? This means there's nothing you can do but accept a situation as it is. This is the Law of Allowing. You can't change the situation, it is what it is, you can't change the person, they are who they are, but you can accept both with allowance.

Fighting back against situations that are out of your control is a useless waste of energy and does not help you grow spiritually. When you involve yourself in campaigns against something, you can draw the thing you're trying to eliminate because you're not allowing it to be what it is by trying to control it. Getting the things we want in life is hard, isn't it? Actually, that's a false statement but most people have been trained to believe it is true. If you believe it's hard to make a lot of money, achieve your dream job, and that everything in life is just hard, hard, hard, it *will be* because you're manifesting it for yourself. But if you live according to the Law of Allowance, the hard things become easy to achieve because you *allow* them to flow to you. So what kind of life would you rather live—a difficult one with many stumbling blocks or one that flows smoothly and easily? I'll choose smooth and easy over hard every time. The Law of Allowing helps you get what you allow to come to you. To live a life where things come easily, you have to focus your attention on allowing everything to happen as it will.

Belief is an essential part of the Law of Allowing. When you believe in something you allow it to enter your life. When you don't believe in something you resist and block it.

Changing from Resistance to Acceptance

Following the Law of Allowing will make your life so much easier because you're changing from resistance to acceptance. I'll give you an example. Growing up, I didn't understand my intuitive abilities. I didn't know why I knew things before they happened and couldn't even begin to explain it in any way except that it completely freaked me out. Every time I tried to make sense of it by sharing what happened to me with someone else, I was made fun of or people thought I was nuts. For a kid, that's not a fun experience. You don't want to feel different from everyone else; instead you want to fit in so I started keeping my mouth shut. I resisted having intuitive abilities for many years. One day I just got tired of trying to hide it. These abilities are part of me, and the more I fought them, the harder life seemed to be. So I stopped fighting. I decided people could choose to like me with my abilities or they could choose not to like me. How they felt about me wasn't something I could change nor was it my problem. It was their issue and part of their life path. Once I allowed myself to accept my abilities as part of my being and stopped worrying about what other people thought of them, life became easier. Since I'd had such a hard time learning how to deal with my own abilities, I decided to help others learn from my experiences. Over the years, this acceptance opened up whole new avenues for teaching, including this book you're reading. But in order to get to this part of my path, I had to allow myself to accept my intuitive nature and release resistance.

The Law of Allowing dictates that you must get out of your own way and *allow* yourself to make more money, have better relationships, and reach all the goals you want to achieve in life. When you allow more to come to you, there is no limit on how much more you will receive. It means changing your feelings from a lack mentality to a positive abundance mentality while believing that you already have what it is you desire. If you feel abundant, you'll be abundant. If you feel successful, you'll be successful. It's all about what you will allow yourself to have and achieve. Don't make things harder than they have to be through resistance. Sure, you've got lessons to learn but life wasn't meant to be a constant fight to get ahead. If you believe that's what you have to do to succeed, then that's what you'll get. But when you change your thoughts and emotions from ones of resistance to allowing then you are truly living the Law of Allowing.

Try It Now

Today be aware of what you're doing. Pay special attention to what you're saying and the actions you're taking. Are you trying to form a situation to fit your needs? Are you being a gossip, busybody, or nosey neighbor? If you find yourself doing any of these things, just stop. Imagine a big, white, mesh sheet floating down from the sky, covering you with lightness and filling you with the calmness of allowing. As the sheet flutters down around you let go of any negative feelings you have, understand that it's not your place to interfere in another person's path, release any feelings of worry or anxiety about things you cannot change. When you feel centered and in balance, then take the sheet off and go about your day minding your own business.

Practical Application Tips

- Are you trying to control a situation? If so, what are you afraid will happen if you just let it be?

- Is a situation directly affecting you in a negative way? If not, then you don't need to be involved.

- Are you trying to resolve something for someone else? Did they ask for your help? If not, let it go.

- Check your resistance levels. If you're resisting instead of allowing, you're creating blocks for yourself.

- Feel the flow of energy within you to allow the universal flow of energy to move through you, bringing positivity and abundance with it.

- Shift your feelings from wanting something to feeling that you already have it.

- Allowing requires openness and acceptance of what you want.

- Universal energy and abundance is always flowing toward you. It's up to you to allow it to happen.

- Leave things alone. Leave people alone. This is allowing.

- When you feel good, happy, and peaceful you are in a state of allowing. If you're angry, frustrated, or annoyed, then you're resisting.

See Also Chapter 39: The Law of Supply and Demand

32

THE LAW OF DISCIPLINE

— ❧ —

I set my priorities high and will remain
disciplined on the path to achievement.

THE LAW OF DISCIPLINE means doing what you know you must do even when you don't want to do it. It is having the mental strength, attitude, and determination to overcome weakness and control your feelings in the pursuit of what you believe to be right even when you are tempted to abandon it. It means not giving up. The Law of Discipline can also be called the Law of Self-Discipline because it is the way you handle yourself, both inside and out, in order to achieve your goals. The concept of discipline can be found in ancient civilizations where great monuments were built, wars fought, and religions started. Today it is an important principal to follow in business and is often one of the prime objectives of entrepreneurs. In the military, discipline is ingrained into its members to achieve goals and hold themselves to higher standards. Discipline will help you with focus, planning, and succeeding. It strengthens your mind, body, and Spirit. No one else can make you disciplined, but if you choose to be, you will be rewarded with a sense of inner power, focus, commitment, independence, and strength of character you can get nowhere else. Discipline comes from within you, from a connection to your spiritual essence and the sense of enlightenment you achieve from the relationship to your true self.

Being disciplined brings with it the opportunity to achieve more in your life, to fulfill your dreams, and create the reality you truly desire. It means you're ready for change and have the willpower, willingness, and desire needed to achieve those changes.

Every day, you're faced with countless decisions that seem insignificant at the time but if looked at as part of a whole, you will see how much you practice the Law of Discipline. Being disciplined means taking on the hard tasks instead of the easy way out. You make difficult decisions and stick by them instead of staying on the fence or remaining undecided.

Avoiding Extremes

Have you ever met someone who is very serious, did everything by the book, is never late, and in total control of every aspect of their life? What about someone who is never on time, feels rules don't apply to them, and seems to never be in control of what is happening in their lives, is very undisciplined, and could be helped by adding some discipline to their lives? There must be balance within the Law of Discipline. Discipline helps you maintain balance through the decisions you make and the actions you take. Just as you go back to your center of energy to find spiritual balance, if you're feeling too rigid or undecided you can give yourself more freedom to be undisciplined in order to bring yourself back into a balanced state.

There are many ways you can become more disciplined through the choices you make. Temptations and distractions can create havoc on discipline. Because we live on the earthly plane, we're always tempted and can be easily distracted. If you are able to remove the thing that is distracting or tempting you, do so. When a distraction can't be easily removed, instead of procrastinating, give yourself a goal to meet and then reward yourself with the distraction. Sometimes a distraction is necessary to keep your mind sharp and focused on the task you need to complete. It's when the temptation or distraction takes all your time away from meeting the goal that it becomes a problem.

Accountability

The Law of Discipline means you hold yourself accountable for your actions. Procrastination only delays what you need to do and can cause negative effects due to the delay. If you had a job where you had to do certain things within a certain timeframe and you continually didn't get the work done in time, you'd no longer have a job. You could make one excuse after another to your boss about why you didn't get the job done, which doesn't matter in the end. You couldn't do the job you were hired to do so the boss has no choice but to relieve you of your duties and find someone else who will get the job done in a timely manner. If you don't hold yourself accountable, someone else might, and it may not be to your benefit. Accountability helps you add structure to your life. It helps you stick to your plans, hold yourself to a higher purpose, and achieve great things.

If you have a hard time adding discipline to your life, then do your hardest task first every day. When you complete the thing you really don't want to do first, then it frees up your day for the things you enjoy. I put items on my list in the order of how much I don't want to do them with the least enjoyable task on top and the most enjoyable one on the bottom. Why? Because I know I'll be tired by the end of the day and if the hardest tasks are already done, the end of my day will be easier. Being disciplined is like a juggling act. You must figure out what works for you and complete all the different things you have to do in a day without dropping the ball. If you have so many things on your plate that you can't get them all done in a day, maybe it's time to let some of it go. When you create a plan for your days, it's easy to get into habits where you can achieve everything you need to do daily. Habits become second nature, requiring little thought. Being unable to stick to your priorities is one of the reasons most people fail to achieve greatness. You must remain dedicated, disciplined, and devoted to your goals in order to fulfill them.

Start Moving to Accomplish More

Newton's law of inertia states that an object at rest stays at rest and an object in motion stays in motion with the same speed and in the same direction unless acted upon by an outside force. Think of yourself as that object and apply the Law of Discipline. It might be hard to get started on a task, but once you're in motion you'll tend to stay in motion until the completion of the task unless an unbalanced force (temptation, distraction, etc.) comes along and knocks you into another direction. It's a natural tendency for objects to keep doing what they're doing once they're in motion. So while it might be hard to get out of bed an hour earlier so you can get a task done, once you're up and working, you'll tend to keep working. It may be difficult to get to the gym, but once you're there, you'll do your workout. So get yourself moving, dig in, and keep the unbalanced forces that interrupt you to a minimum. You'll see yourself making great strides toward what you want in life.

Being disciplined is a strength you can call upon at any point in your life to keep yourself on track and get the job done. Each person has unique talents they use to reach their goals. The most successful people also have the discipline to put in the time required to reach those goals. They're able to rely on the strength inside themselves that makes them practice long hours to become a great violinist or run for miles and miles to become an Olympic track and field gold medalist. As an observer you may only see end results, the successful completion of another person's goal and not all the hard work that went into the achievement. Discipline and dedication can make all the difference in the world between being average and achieving greatness. Anything you want to do or achieve is possible through living the Law of Discipline. It makes you happier and more fulfilled because you've seen something through to the end through focus, determination, and devotion to ultimately achieve success. If you want it, set your mind to it, be disciplined in your approach, be persistent and don't give up, and eventually it will be yours.

Try It Now

When it comes to discipline, it's important to always finish what you start. If you leave tasks incomplete, then you're creating a lot of loose ends for yourself. What tasks have you left incomplete? Write them all down and then put all your focus on completing them. As you do, you'll gain a sense of fulfillment, of completion. Discipline can keep you from creating messy loose ends that can hold you back from moving forward.

Practical Application Tips

- Get regular exercise to increase your mental performance, sleep quality, and improve your willpower. If you discipline yourself to get some type of exercise every day you'll feel better overall.

- Easy success is usually a myth. That doesn't mean it can't happen but 99.9% of the time success is achieved through a disciplined approach and hard work over time.

- If you wait until you feel like doing something it may never get done. Do it now, whether you feel like it or not.

- Refrain from doing mindless tasks that are simply for your own amusement when the time could be spent working towards your goals.

- Distractions and temptations can derail your progress toward success. Try to keep them to a minimum. Only allow them to recharge yourself or as a reward for work completed.

- Excuses will not get you to your goal. Eliminate them from your life.

- Create an external deadline for yourself. One you've shared with someone else or where others are depending on you to deliver something to them by a certain date. Then you're more likely to reach your goal on time.

- Set active goals for yourself. Write them down, make yourself accountable for them, and then get it done.

- Ignore those who don't believe in you. You know how disciplined you are and you will achieve your goals regardless of what others do to sidetrack you.

- Get on task to stay on task. The hardest part is getting started.

See Also Chapter 35: The Law of Patience

33

THE LAW OF CYCLES

—🕊—

Whether up or down, I will flow with the
cycle of my life to become all that I am capable of
being and achieve all that is mine in this lifetime.

THE LAW OF CYCLES states the universe is made of energy that runs in currents, in cycles, ebbs and flows, vibrating at different rates at different times. Because of this nature of universal energy, events in life will also follow a regularly repeated sequence of events. Within every cycle there will be increases and decreases offset by times of stabilization in between. Times of increase have greater momentum and projects launched during those times have a greater chance of success. Scientifically, this is well-documented in nature, making the seasons a great case in point regarding the flow of cycles and is an example of how we can use cycles to aid us. Spring is a time of rebirth, warmth, growth, and increase that gains momentum then levels off during the summer and then starts decreasing in the fall until it levels off again in winter, a time of hibernation, dormancy, and cold. People have survived harsh winters because they had enough food by planting in the spring and harvesting in the fall throughout history.

The Law of Cycles is an easy law to take for granted. We see it every day and never think anything about it while enjoying the sunrise and sunset, the seasons of the year, the phases of the moon or the flow of the tides. Even our own heartbeat and breathing follows a cycle. If you look at anything in nature, you'll find the rise and fall of cycles in the world. As a spiritual being you'll go through cycles where everything is going great and then just as suddenly it seems like everything is falling apart. This is natural.

Recognition of Your Cycles

Recognizing the cycles in your life can help you take advantage of them as you aim for success. If you've just gone though a time of increase and are in the period of stabilization, then you know that a time of decrease is on the way and you can get ready for it. Awareness is critical when dealing with cycles. If you're unaware of when a cycle is starting then you can't plan accordingly. Have you ever gotten busy during a summer day and before you realize it, dusk has arrived and the mosquitoes are having a picnic on you? Because you were busy, you lost track of time, were unprepared for the change in the cycle from day to night, and the bugs that come out at night. Had you been aware and prepared, you could have applied mosquito spray prior to dusk and been protected from their bites.

As you make plans, wait until the most favorable part of any cycle in order to give it the best possible chance of success. Think of the retail industry. You'll find clothing and products on sale that coincide with the seasons. You're not going to find summer products in the middle of winter or vice versa because they simply aren't going to sell. Specific product placement coinciding with the season guarantees more sales because that's when the product is needed. If your goal is to sell something you created, pick the season where it will be used the most and launch the product then. Anytime a cycle is moving in downward motion or is in a time of decrease, wait until it moves back into a time of increase and rising energy for the best chance at success. Our frequency ebbs and flows just like the energy within the rest of the universe. When you're able to get in tune with your own unique energy cycle, you can determine when your frequency is elevating and when it is decreasing. Being aware of your individual energetic flow can help you live in harmony with your spiritual self and universal energy. There is a time for everything in life. If you feel the time isn't right, or that you should wait, then don't jump the gun and move forward anyway. Listen to your intuition, instincts, and higher self and wait a while on whatever it is you planned to do. When the time is right, you'll know it in your heart, you'll feel it in your energy, and you'll be drawn to take action by the pull of universal energy. There's nothing wrong with waiting, even if others are urging you to take action.

Within your life you'll encounter many types of cycles. In your career you may have many different jobs before settling on one that fits you just right, or you may have planned for a given profession and gone to school for it only to discover that you truly dislike the work, which brings about a career change. A hobby you love may turn into a multi-million-dollar corporation, or properties you owned and then sold turned a great profit for you. Personal changes often usher out the old while bringing in the new, allowing you to embark on a new avenue of your spiritual path. The Law of Cycles can help you flow with these changes, bringing enlightenment, new creativity, and harmony.

Cycles of the People in Your Life

People also cycle through your life. Over time, some of the close friends you had in high school may no longer be part of your life. Now you have new friends and you will have even more in the future. People come and go in our lives. Some friends are with you forever, and sometimes they're only in your life for a short while before moving in a different direction. There are always reasons for their appearance in your life so enjoy their friendship and find the lessons that they will teach you when they are in it. We are all growing, changing, and moving through both the times of increase, decrease, and stabilization associated with the Law of Cycles. Everything and everyone changes. When you're able to move in harmony with these changes instead of remaining stuck in the past then you're in forward motion.

It's how we handle the difficulties that enable us to experience strength of character, personal, and spiritual growth. Once things start to calm down for you, the next thing to expect is for everything to start looking up. So instead of complaining, crying, and whining when you're in the decrease phase, think positively and start planning for the stabilization and increase part of the cycle. Instead, as difficult as it can be to do so during hard times, try to look past the current problems and remain positive, upbeat, and look forward to the great things that will come to you once this part of the cycle passes.

Growing up in a farming family, planting crops and harvesting them were done according to the change of seasons, when frosts were expected and the phases of the moon. By looking at the cycles in nature and knowing when things were expected to happen, we were able to plan accordingly to reap the most volume from the crops, which was then canned and stored for the cycle of decrease (Winter). That way, there would be food for the family during the dormant season. When you're able to track a cycle like you do with planting and harvesting, it makes it easier to see the results of your efforts. You may work extremely hard during the time of increase but then you're well prepared for the time of decrease. You can plan situations in your own life in the same way by examining them and determining where you are in your cycle. Is this a good time to start a new project or relationship? If you're in the increase part of your individual cycle, then of course it is! But if you feel like you're in the time of decrease, maybe it's better to wait a bit to plant the seeds of a relationship when you know it will take root, grow, bloom, and produce fruit like plants do in the spring.

Knowing how the Law of Cycles works will enable you to make clearer plans for your life so you can achieve the most success possible. It may take a little work to have a clear vision of where you are in your unique cycle but once known, anything is possible.

Try It Now

To determine where you are in the cycle of increase/decrease examine what has been going on in your life lately. You may be able to automatically say, it's going great or it's going badly. If everything is going great then you're in the increase part of the cycle, if things are problematic, then you're in the decrease phase. If you're uncertain because you're experiencing both good and problematic situations, write a list of pros and cons to see where you are. You may be in the period of stabilization or on the cusp of the decrease phase to the increase phase or vice versa. Make notes to refer back to or start a cycle journal to help you determine your own cycles, how long each phase lasts, and the things that happen during each phase. It's great information to have on hand if you take the time to create it. This will help you move with the cycles instead of against them.

Practical Application Tips
- Make plans during the stabilization and decrease phases.

- Start new projects during the increase phase.

- Track your own unique cycle to have better control over your decision making process.

- There is a time for everything.

- If you need to change your plans and wait, then do that. There's nothing wrong with holding back if you feel the time isn't right. There's nothing worse than ignoring your intuition, and then having circumstances prove that your intuition to wait was correct.

- Become aware of both spiritual cycles and the cycles in the natural world when making plans.

- Appreciate the people in your life while they're in it.

- Don't take the Law of Cycles for granted, instead, use it to make the most of your life.

- When you're in the decrease phase, don't give up hope. Stay positive, make plans, and look forward to the increase phase.

See Also Chapter 24: The Law of Sacrifice

34

THE LAW OF PROSPERITY

— 🕊 —

Today I will feel joy, happiness, and elation for prosperity experienced by those I know and myself.

THE LAW OF PROSPERITY states that when one person prospers, we all prosper in direct proportion to the happiness you feel for the other person's prosperity or your own. The Law of Prosperity means embracing universal abundance and leaving behind an attitude of lack. Prosperity is a wide-reaching term. It's origins in Buddhism and Christianity connect it with spirituality and collectivism. In business it's connected with earning a profit and being financially successful. Most people automatically think of money when they think of being prosperous but it's much more than that; it is success and good fortune in any aspect of life. If you can feel positive emotions about someone else's success then that's prosperity.

The Law of Prosperity means feeling happy for another's good fortune regardless of our own situation.

Sounds simple, right? It is as long as you don't let negative emotions such as jealousy and envy intrude on your feelings about the other person's happiness with their success. Anytime you're successful, your frequency elevates. You're filled with feelings of happiness, joy, and fulfillment because you accomplished what you set out to do. When you're happy for someone's success, your frequency matches their own, which in turn will bring prosperity to you.

How Emotions Affect Prosperity

The opposite—feeling happiness for someone else—also follows this law. If you are jealous of the other person's success, if you create scenarios in your mind based on how you think the other person may act because of their newly found success, increase in money, or new purchase; you're creating negativity for yourself. Or if you're taking pleasure in another person's failures, that's blocking your own prosperity potential. Both reflect fears, a sense of lack, or jealousy. Once you address these types of issues within yourself, you can feel joy for another's accomplishments. Prosperity doesn't mean taking from another, it means enjoying the abundance the universe gives to you and everyone else. Allow yourself to take pleasure in the success of others so you can draw prosperity to yourself and feel happiness for your own success when it comes.

It's important to be aware of your emotions when you experience prosperity. If someone else is trying to make you feel guilty or undeserving of your success, don't let them. If you achieve it, own it; be proud of your accomplishment and yourself for being able to obtain success and prosperity. If someone doesn't like it, that's their problem, not yours. It's not your responsibility, nor should you feel bad about the positive things you are able to achieve in life.

Not everyone strives to achieve more and more in life. If you're happy, content, and satisfied with the way your life is at this moment in time, then the universe rewards you by giving you more of the things that keep you happy in your prosperity. There's absolutely nothing wrong with wanting to do well and achieve more, but at some point you have to experience contentment and satisfaction, otherwise you're just a hamster on a wheel, never stopping to enjoy the things you've achieved. When you do, and appreciate what you have, then you'll discover even more abundance comes your way.

When you are generous and giving, you will always be prosperous. You can give of your time, money, creativity, you can give things to others that you no longer need, you can give unexpected surprises (always fun), or lend an ear or shoulder. By being open to share your true spiritual nature with others in a positive way, you're opening space in your own life to receive something new to fill that space and increasing your frequency to match the abundance coming to you.

Prosperity and the Subconscious Mind

Our subconscious mind picks up on key words to manifest what we desire, so we must make sure our primary thought is one of prosperity. Keep words like *don't* or *can't* out of your vocabulary because your subconscious mind will grab hold of that negative word and block whatever it is you want from coming to you. For example, if you said "I don't have enough money for that car" then your subconscious mind will agree and keep you from obtaining enough money for the car. But if you say, "I'm going to own the car soon because I'm saving money for it" then your subconscious mind agrees and will bring more money to you so you can save to buy the car. Having a prosperity consciousness means thinking in the positive with powerful words, which will bring you what you need. Your thoughts must be clear and concise.

Sometimes you're not exactly sure what it is you want or how you're going to achieve it. If you're meandering from one thing to another without set goals or a plan of how you will achieve those goals, your subconscious mind can't manifest your desires. If one or the other of these is missing, there isn't enough forward focus and you end up doing your daily activities instead of striving toward a prosperous goal. If you are in this type of rut, it's a good time to really think about what prosperity means to you. What do you really want to achieve? How can you bring it into your life? Decide and then put a plan into action. Your subconscious mind will be happy to help you get to where you want to be and attain what you want but you must know what that is first.

Sometimes you may not feel that you deserve the prosperity you want to attain. This can be from guilt, listening to someone who doesn't want to see you succeed, or because you feel you're always spinning your wheels and getting nowhere. Maybe money was always hard to come by in the past. When there isn't enough money, you worry about spending too much or how you will ration it to make it last longer. So when you are earning more money, if you don't adjust your mindset along with the increase, then you end up blocking yourself from making even more money. Instead of worrying about what other people will think when you're earning more, or if they will change how they interact with you, just feel blessed in your achievements and don't treat them any differently than you do now. If they choose to act differently to you, then you can deal with it at that time. By worrying about something that hasn't happened yet, you're setting up blocks to prevent you from achieving the success you want.

Prosperity Brings Change

Prosperity in any form always brings some kind of change with it. Be willing to flow with the change in order to be truly prosperous. Will you make new friends and leave old ones behind? Maybe, maybe not. You can't let fear of change hold you back from being all you want to be. If you let fear rule you then you're not living your true purpose. Put fear of change and how others will react to the changes happening to you aside while focusing on your path to prosperity. This takes bravery and a thick skin. It will strengthen your character and you'll see who really likes or loves you for you and who lets their own fear affect how they treat you.

Gaining prosperity in your life can be hard work. For some, the required time, energy, devotion, and amount of work may be too much, such that ultimately these people decide they don't want to make their lives any different than it is right now. It's easier to sit back and take life as it comes instead of going for the gusto. And that's completely fine. To be financially prosperous, you might have to put in long hours at your job to move up the career ladder. If you start your own business, it's up to you to make it a success, requiring dedication, conviction, and an unfaltering belief that you will be successful. When all your work pays off and you're making an excellent income and enjoying the things in life that financial prosperity can bring, you'll look back on the road traveled and know it was worth it if earning more money is one of your goals.

Only you can decide how much prosperity you want in your life and what you're willing to do to achieve it. If you want more money, more happiness, or more of anything, then you must reach out and get it instead of sitting back and waiting for it to come to you. Always remember that the happiness you feel for another person's success will bring prosperity back to you tenfold.

Try It Now

To determine how you feel about prosperity think of the last time you received something good in your life. How did you feel? Were you happy but then started to feel undeserving or guilty for receiving prosperity? Or did you welcome it with open arms never feeling guilt or other negative emotions? Be honest with yourself. If you felt any negative feelings associated with receiving good fortune, then you need to determine why you felt that way so you can address it and release it. Now think of someone else you know who experienced prosperity in their lives. How did you feel about it? Were you happy for them? Or were you secretly irritated and annoyed they got something that you didn't? If so, address these feelings to move to a more prosperous state.

Practical Application Tips

- Be happy for someone else when they are successful.

- Leave jealousy, envy, and resentment behind.

- Embrace an abundance mentality and prosperity consciousness.

- Move beyond a lack mentality or poverty consciousness to bring more prosperity to your life.

- Worrying about what other people will think about your success will only hold you back from achieving that success. Let it go.

- Know you deserve to be prosperous. Own it.

- Change will always happen when you're living the Law of Prosperity. Expect it and flow with it.

- Prosperity requires hard work. If you're not willing to work for it you may not really want it.

- How prosperous you are is up to you.

- Hoarding tells the universe that you don't need more so it will stop flowing to you.

See Also Chapter 16: The Law of Success

35

THE LAW OF PATIENCE

— ❧ —

*Today I will practice patience in all I do. I will see
situations from another's point of view and refrain
from losing my mind over things I can't control.*

THE LAW OF PATIENCE states that all things will happen when the time
is right for them to fulfill their purpose in your life. It means things will
not be rushed, the universe works in its own timeframe, which is often
much slower than ours. You can't rush success, happiness, enlightenment, financial independence, or anything else you're trying to achieve
in life. The idea that patience is a virtue can be traced back to the poem
The Vision of Piers Plowman which was written by William Langland
between 1360 and 1387.

Patience is your ability to wait, be tolerant and endure difficult situations, especially when those situations cause lateness or delays, without

feeling annoyance, anxiety, anger, or frustration. Everything will happen in the right time. It doesn't matter how mad or upset you get because the situation is making you late, or how much you complain or say ugly things to other people, you can't change how time moves or how the situation will develop. To be successful in life, you need to have patience.

I used to be the world's worst when it came to losing my patience. I'm a red-headed Scorpio of Scot-Irish heritage—I kind of have the odds of keeping a cool head stacked against me! When I was younger I lost my temper quite often until one day when I was late to work. I was frustrated and mad because of the delays that had kept me from getting there on time. I have a thing about being late and feel it is irresponsible to not arrive on time. But that day, I had an eye-opening experience. I was stuck in heavy traffic and when it finally started moving, I passed the accident site—the car in the wreck was a red Honda Civic, just like my car. When I saw that, I also heard a voice say *That could have been you.* Suddenly it washed over me that the reason I had been uncharacteristically late was because someone on the spiritual plane was watching out for me, throwing little obstacles in my path to slow me down so I wasn't on that part of the highway at the time of the accident but a little bit later. I felt really horrible for the people in the accident but also couldn't help but be thankful for my guides' help in slowing me down and making sure I understood the lesson. Today, I don't lose my patience very often because I know there is a reason behind the changes in my life. When things get tough and my patience wears thin, I just remember that maybe someone is watching out for me again.

Learning Patience

Sometimes it can be difficult to be patient, especially when your emotions have gotten away from you. If that happens, try to bring yourself to center, and find your balance again. Try to think of the situation from the other person's point of view. The lady in front of you in the checkout line isn't purposefully trying to irritate you because she's counting out her change to pay for her purchase. Maybe she is embarrassed because she has to pay in coins. That kid crying his eyes out isn't doing it because he knows a crying kid gets on your nerves. Maybe he has stomach cramps and is in pain but is too young to say he's hurting so all he can do is cry. Or the driver who suddenly slammed on the brakes didn't do it so you'd hit them, but was trying to avoid hitting another car that pulled out in front of them. When you only look at what's making you lose your patience from your own point of view, it's easy to let negative emotions take control. But when you take the time to look at it from another's point of view, then it's easier to remain patient and let things happen as they will.

Losing patience can teach lessons. If you're always late and impatient with the drivers on the way to work, you can easily solve the problem by leaving your house earlier. Look for solutions on your end to help you be more patient and understanding. You can learn a lot about yourself by examining how you handle situations where a little patience could go a long way. Are you being rigid, intolerant, and unforgiving when it comes to an unexpected delay? If you were more flexible, tolerant, and forgiving, then maybe you wouldn't lose your temper. Being patient can also help you make better decisions. When you take time to look at a situation from multiple points of view then you're less likely to make the wrong decision because you didn't take time to think it through.

Patience is a powerful skill you can learn. It's all about managing your emotions, timing your reactions and actions so they will have the greatest positive effect to help you attain what you want. When you learn how to be patient, how to wait your turn, and how to see the bigger picture, then you have more power and control over your life. Being impatient leads to rash actions you might regret later, while being patient enables you to think things through, make wise decisions, and take the appropriate action.

Practicing Patience

So if you tend to be impatient, how can you become more patient? You have to figure out what sets you off. Does a slow driver put you in a rage? Does waiting in line cause you to lose your mind? Once you know what triggers your impatience you can do something about it. If you know waiting in long lines sets you off, then either pick the shortest line you can find or come back to do the task another day. If you can't come back another day, resolve yourself to waiting and do something mentally until it's your turn. Once when I found myself getting annoyed at the length of time I had to wait, I started counting the ceiling tiles. You might think that's silly but it gave my mind something to do, it distracted me from the time I was having to wait and by the time I'd gotten to two-hundred, it was my turn. I've also chosen to read the labels on the groceries, or even start a conversation with someone else in line with me about something totally unrelated to having to wait.

Different people have different signs that let them know when they're about to blow. You may start sweating, gritting your teeth, feeling irritable or short-tempered, or start taking short shallow breaths. Just as you figured out what triggers impatience for you, figure out the signs you start to show when you're about to lose your patience. By doing this you can prevent it.

Patience can help you become stress free, have a better, happier attitude, feel more powerful and self-confident. It can help you turn negatives into positives, sadness into happiness, and bring to life more than you ever imagined possible. Not only will you treat yourself better when you're patient, but you'll treat others better as well because you will be more compassionate. It will be easier to accept situations as they happen without starting a fight about it. Better yet, if you use creative visualization you can foresee any future problems and plan accordingly to prevent them from happening.

Practicing the Law of Patience changes how others view you. Have you ever seen an impatient person and thought they seemed arrogant, as if their issue was the only one at hand? I have and it's not fun dealing with those types of people because they can be insensitive to everyone else's feelings but their own. It's very difficult to achieve goals when you're acting like this and pushing people away, even people who could potentially help you accomplish your goals. Learn to practice patience so you can get along well with others, understand multiple points of view, achieve all you desire, and be in harmony with yourself and everything happening around you.

Try It Now

A good way to learn to practice patience is through your breathing. If you find yourself feeling stressed, frazzled, or on edge, take a moment to monitor yourself through deep breaths. You can be standing, sitting, or in the middle of doing anything when you do this exercise. Anytime you're aware that your mood isn't the best it could be or that you're short on patience, take a deep breath. As you slowly inhale imagine the air filled with calming white light, on the exhale imagine all the stress, anxiety and frustration leaving your system. Do this multiple times until you feel calmness settling over you, restoring your ability to be patient. Once you feel more centered and balanced, continue with whatever you were doing.

Practical Application Tips

- Everything happens in the time it is supposed to happen. Sometimes I have to wait.

- When you feel like you're going to lose your patience take several long deep breaths, focus on your inner essence and spiritual sense of balance to bring yourself back to center and keep your patience in check.

- I will let go of the things that make me impatient so I can regain my composure and patience.

- I will not be selfish but will look at the needs and situations of others to help me remain patient with them.

- I need to practice patience to be successful. No one wants to hire, promote, or partner with someone who is impatient.

- Patience builds character and builds a positive self-image within me and in the eyes of my family, friends, and business associates.

- Patience helps me remember what matters in life.

- I will achieve my goals when the time is right through hard work and patience.

- Timing is everything.

- I will not be too hard on myself if I lose my patience. I will just regroup and get myself back on track.

See Also Chapter 32: The Law of Discipline

36

THE LAW OF AWAKENING

— ✣ —

*Today I am aware of my being, my surroundings,
and the people I interact with in order to awaken
to that which will enable my growth and success.*

THE LAW OF AWAKENING states that in order to experience an awakening whether spiritual, personal or in any other aspect of your life, you have to become more aware, and to achieve awareness you must maintain self-control, stability, and focus. This law is often also called the Law of Awareness or the Law of Spiritual Awakening, but because I believe that an awakening can happen in any aspect of your life, so I prefer the Law of Awakening. The idea of awareness is an integral part of Taoism, Buddhism, and Shamanism because you need awareness in order to work with Spirit.

What happens when you physically wake up after sleeping? You become aware of your surroundings, even if you don't immediately open your eyes. If you fell asleep on the bow of a boat, you'd hear the splash of the water, feel the rocking of the boat, the sun on your skin, and the hardness of the boat under your back. You may hear birds, other people talking or other boat engines. Eventually you are completely awake and aware of your reality, where you are, and what you're doing. When we experience an awakening, it happens the same way. We become aware of little things first, then the more we experience the truth of situations we're in or change our way of thinking, we become more fully aware until we're completely awake.

The Law of Awakening means to be aware of both the positive and the negative in life, to see the past, present, and future, to look at potential successes and potential failures. It means to consider everything in order to have a fuller understanding of the whole as you acknowledge other states of awareness. Awakening means opening to new opportunities, seeing things differently than you have in the past, and using this new knowledge to expand your consciousness, to find yourself in a more awakened state of mind.

Spiritual Awakening

Spiritually speaking, to experience an awakening means you observe, experience, and are attentive to the existence of things you may not have previously known or understood but yet do not deny. In a spiritual awakening you may begin to question who you are and your purpose for being on the earthly plane. You recognize there is more within you than just your physical body, you may remember bits and pieces of past lives, or you become aware of your intuition. Many times right before a spiritual awakening, you will go through a traumatic or life altering experience that acts as a catalyst to your waking up that makes you question everything you previously believed. You will begin to let go of that which no longer serves you, the negativity of the past will no longer have ties over you so you let that go too, and, it enables you to gain clarity of purpose. You will have more déjà vu moments and other synchronicities that let you know you're now walking your spiritual path and living your purpose. With a spiritual awakening, you see past the physical to the Divine. There is calmness, a lightness of being, associated with your new understanding that love is at the center of your existence, which enables you to release fear.

When you experience a spiritual awakening it usually begins because you're questioning things about life and start seeking answers that resonate with you. I know for me I started searching for my own truth after people in a church I attended started treating me differently outside of church. It just didn't make sense to me so I began to look deeper into spirituality primarily to try to find a way to understand my own intuition, which at the time didn't make sense to me either. As my awakening continued, I'd find the content in many metaphysical books just felt right to me. It allowed me to see different paths I could take to gain the things I wanted to achieve because I was now more aware than ever before and looked to the positive instead of focusing on the negatives. Add in the paranormal experiences which made me question everything I thought I knew, and I woke up even more. Your own awakening may be started by a life event, something you read, or a feeling that there was more to your purpose than what you currently thought.

Awakening Awareness

In order to achieve the things you want in life you have to understand the awareness part of the Law of Awakening. If you're not aware of the things that happen or need to happen in order to achieve what you want, then they can be harder to obtain. When you learn to be more observant, watchful, and attentive, when you increase your awareness through research, discussions, or working in a similar situation, then you're opening your eyes to the possibilities out there for you. It is important to understand that when you experience an awakening of any sort, you have to know yourself so you can put into practice what you've awakened. You can have the best product in the world, but it could flop if you don't market it correctly. If you awaken to the spiritual world and realize there is unlimited abundance waiting for you but do nothing to try to obtain it, you're not fully using the information you've been given. When you awaken to anything in life it is because it's part of your master plan for your earthly experience. Through awakening you can connect to the spiritual part of your being, achieve what you desire, and create abundance in your life.

Another part of the awakening process is realizing how another's actions or inaction affects what you're doing or what you're trying to achieve. You are able to see potential problems before they develop so you can take steps to prevent them. On the other hand, you can also see potential successes and strategically plan for them. Being awakened means living in the moment, accepting new information, and understanding a greater plan than you've considered before. It means your awareness of everything happening around you is heightened. You feel more, sense more, and understand more. As you adjust to each period of awakening you go through there will be a time frame where everything is clear. But then over time as you adjust to being on this different level of awareness, it becomes second nature. The same thing happens with each period of awakening.

There are other signs indicative of an awakening: you may suddenly feel you're trapped in your job, that there are too many negative people around you, your lifestyle is no longer holding appeal and you suddenly want to completely change it, or you feel like you just need to break free from the mundane and experience the exceptional. Sometimes you're suddenly faced with having to deal with unresolved issues from the past. This is part of the clearing out of negativity that happens during an awakening. Find a way to resolve the issue so you can move on. I would often experience vivid and prophetic dreams or feel like I needed to hurry up and do something because time was running out to get it done. Sometimes the dreams and feelings were connected; other times I couldn't find a connection. After years of never having anyone to explain the intuitive or paranormal things I experienced, once I started my spiritual awakening, it seemed like there were teachers everywhere. I wasn't looking for them but they found me and gave me new insights on my path. Being more aware of what was happening made me appreciate them and helped me better understand the whole experience.

An awakening allows you to feel inner harmony, it increases abundance in your life, and will help you be successful. During a period of awakening you'll notice you're exceptionally observant, especially of yourself, your actions and reactions. You become more aware of your thoughts, especially new ideas you haven't considered before, but which now feel like they connect with you. It's important during this time to make sure you're not overthinking everything. Sometimes it's easy to analyze things too much, which can hinder your progress. During a time of awakening, you'll feel more independent, secure in your beliefs and the path you should take, and confident in your choices, decisions, and actions.

Try It Now

Becoming more observant and aware is a way you can actively participate in your awakening. Here are some steps you can take to increase your awareness to help you in your achievements. In any situation pay attention to what other people are doing. Pay attention to what they say, plans they're making and how they are going about achieving their goals. You may learn something from them that will help you achieve your own. Notice any patterns that occur in your life and evaluate how you can become more successful. Look for unexpected changes and be constantly aware of your daily interactions with people as well as how others interact with one another. Observing human nature can be very enlightening. Learn to remain silent when it is needed and to speak when appropriate. Sometimes you can learn more by keeping quiet then you can by talking. While you don't have to write any of this down, sometimes making notes about your observations can help you with your own awakening or your plan to achieve your desires.

Practical Application Tips

- Make an effort to become more aware of your own mind, body, and Spirit.

- Know yourself and whether you are willing to take the actions needed to achieve what you want.

- Be an observer of human nature.

- Don't be judgmental.

- Watch, listen, and learn.

- When a teacher appears, accept the help with love and gratitude.

- Look for triggers that mean you are in a state of awakening.

- Question yourself, your beliefs, and your intentions.

- If new ideas resonate with you, make them part of your being.

- Live in the moment while letting go of negativity of the past.

See Also Chapter 15: The Law of Clarity

37

THE LAW OF CAUSE AND EFFECT

*I choose to create positive catalysts in my life
to receive awesome effects as a universal reward.*

THE LAW OF CAUSE and Effect states that every action (cause) has a consequence (effect). Your thoughts, actions, and reactions (causes) create the consequences (effects), and these effects must physically manifest in your current reality. You may have heard the Law of Cause and Effect stated as reaping what you sow, there are consequences for your actions, or for every action there is an equal and opposite reaction (Sir Isaac Newton's Third Law of Motion). In the *Kybalion* it is written as: "Every Cause has its Effect; every Effect has its Cause; everything happens according to Law; Chance is but a name for Law not recognized; there are many planes of causation, but nothing escapes the Law."

The Law of Cause and Effect means everything you do is a catalyst for a wave of energy to go from your frequency, your spiritual energy, out into the universe and then to bring the effect of that catalyst back to you. It doesn't matter if the effect is positive or negative, conscious or unconscious—it will come back in time. Because this law deals with the effects of energy, which is continually changing, you have the ability to use this flow of energy to change your life for the better.

You can also look at the Law of Cause and Effect as justice from the universe for your thoughts and behaviors. While the law itself is neutral and doesn't make distinctions regarding good and bad, working with cause and effect brings together energy that is drawn toward one another. Helping others, being a trustworthy person, and offering random acts of kindness are all ways we can send out good energy into our realities. When we are aware that everything we do sets off an energetic chain reaction, then it enables us to look further down the road at what the potential results of our actions could be. When we look ahead, it can help us make better decisions before we take action.

Energy in Motion

Everything within the universe is constantly changing because universal energy is always in motion. There is always a cause and effect, even if we can't see it. Even when you're not consciously aware of the events you set in action by the things you do and say, they still have an effect. It's important to think before you speak, especially when you're angry, because words have power. Being focused and attentive to your thoughts and actions enable you to live in the moments of your life so be aware of the catalysts you're sending out. Growth occurs with change. Otherwise we'd all live in a stagnant rut without new and exciting things happening to us.

The Law of Cause and Effect can emotionally affect many people because it works like a chain reaction. If you're having a great day then the catalyst of your vibrant energy will rub off on others who may be experiencing a difficult day, which can make their day brighter. Or if you're in a bad mood, then your mood can rub off on others just as easily. Think of a time when you went into work in a great mood and then by the time the day was over you felt stressed and frustrated because everyone else was in an irritable mood. It's easy to allow the emotions of others to negatively affect you, especially if you're an empath, but it doesn't have to if you choose not to attract their energy to you. By allowing your energy to stay positive and by having a good outlook on situations, you can counteract the negativity others are sending out because higher level frequencies offset lower level frequencies. You can choose to be part of the crowd who allows others to control how they're feeling or you can choose to rise above the cause and effect manipulations of others to control your own destiny. This is a must if you're going to be successful in life, in business, or in obtaining the things you want.

Catalysts to Action

Nothing happens without a reason. What you're experiencing now, at this moment, instigated at some point in your past due to the thoughts you had or actions you took. If your life isn't going the way you want it to, you can change it by creating catalysts that will bring good things to you. Now, it's not going to happen overnight. You're going to have to keep working at creating positive catalysts but in time you will see positive effects show up in your life.

Not taking action or ignoring potential opportunities will have the same effect as a negative catalyst. Many people don't want to get involved in situations or they sit on the fence because they don't want to make a decision. Inaction is like spinning your wheels in the mud, you're not going forward because you choose not to take action.

There is never a time when the Law of Cause and Effect isn't working. Think about that for a moment. Every minute of every day people will experience the effects of the things they cause based on their thoughts and actions. Universal energy will never change. If it never changes in its flow, you have to learn to flow with its positivity or you will flow against it.

Let's take a few minutes to look at some life situations to see cause and effect. If you're having problems saving money is it because you're spending too much? Is that weight set or bike in the corner collecting dust because you aren't allotting the necessary time for a workout? Is the house a mess because you're procrastinating and not cleaning it up? Each of these things is a result of the catalyst you put out because of your thoughts and actions. You deserve to buy lots of stuff right? It's your money; you can do what you want with it. And it's no big deal if you wait to work out or clean up tomorrow, is it? If you want to save money you'll have to tighten your belt and stop over spending. If you want to improve your health and physique then you have to work out. If you want to live in a nice environment you have to clean up. Anything you want, you have to put a catalyst out there for it to come to you, but you also need to take specific actions to obtain what you want. In other words, you have to do the work to achieve. It's going to come back to you anyway, but why not help it along a bit so it happens faster?

You can apply the Law of Cause and Effect to business, relationships, career paths, or anything you want to do. How? You look at what successful people have done in the past to achieve the same results. If you follow their example and take the same steps you should be able to achieve the same results, however, if you skip steps or do something differently your results will not be exactly the same, they could be less or they could be better. There are lots of people who want to share their success with others. They want you to be able to achieve the same positive results they did so they offer to teach you how they did it in order to help you do it too. If it's something you really want to achieve, find a mentor who can help you learn the steps to take to be successful. Remember achieving success takes time, effort, and desire on your part.

Don't expect to become an overnight success but if it does come quickly be appreciative and enjoy it.

Try It Now

Tear a piece of aluminum foil from a roll. Lay it flat on the counter and then put several drops of water on it. Lift the edges and tilt the foil first one way then the other. Look at how easily the water droplets travel from side to side. Nothing impedes the flow. Let the water flow off of the foil and then crush the foil into a tight ball. Now spread it out and get it as flat as you can. Put more water drops on the foil, lift and tilt it. What happens? The little crinkles in the foil now alter the flow of water. It no longer moves easily from one side to the other but instead must flow over the ridges and creases. This is the Law of Cause and Effect in action. Before you took action and balled up the foil, the energy of the water moved freely, just as universal energy moves freely around us all of the time. But the action you took changed the foil, making it more difficult to navigate, similar to challenges we experience in life. Now the energy of the water has to work harder to move from side to side, going over obstacles in its way and sometimes running back into itself. This is the effect of the action of balling up the foil. Think of your life as the foil. If you feel like you're receiving too much negativity coming back to you, start fresh with a new piece of foil, and only take positive actions that will keep the surface clean and flat. Do all you can to keep your experience smooth and free of obstacles so the energy flows effortless and in positivity.

Practical Application Tips

- Don't let yourself get dragged into another person's negativity.
- Success comes from within you.
- Luck, chance, and twists of fate will not determine your success.

- Your thoughts, actions, and reactions will determine whether you receive positive or negative effects.

- Choose to have a good, positive attitude to create success in your life.

- You create the causes in your life; the universe gives you the effects.

- You can turn your life around any time you choose through the creation of positive catalysts that return positive results.

- The interpretation of your reality is up to you.

- Focus on making the cause positive and the effect will return as the same.

See Also Chapter 7: The Law of Attraction

38

THE LAW OF BALANCE AND POLARITY

— 🕊 —

*Today I will look at situations from a different
perspective so I do not act in the extreme.*

THE LAW OF BALANCE and Polarity, also known as the Law of Symmetry or the Law of Duality, states there is a polarity between all things within the universe; between those extreme opposites, balance is found. This law plays out in scientific observation, in business practices, and within us on mental and physical levels. Finding balance in all areas of our lives is the ultimate goal, but in order to get there, we must experience both sides of the polar opposites, the extremes of the same thing in varying degrees, in order to understand what balance feels like.

According to the *Kybalion*, "everything is dual; everything has poles; everything has its pair of opposites; like and unlike are the same; opposites are identical in nature, but different in degree; extremes meet; all truths are but half-truths; all paradoxes may be reconciled." A good example of this is the weather. I live in south Florida which has a tropical climate. One minute it can be hot and sunny with a slight breeze, a few minutes later a severe lightning storm can roll though. The sun and the storms are both varying degrees of the same thing—weather. If you live where it gets cold you also experience this. It'll be hot in summer and cold in winter. This might seem like opposites at first but the heat and cold are just opposite ends of the same spectrum of temperature. This polarity applies to everything in the universe. Your love life, relationships, career, and emotions are all affected. You can't have light without darkness, good without evil, peace without struggle, or positive without negative. These are each opposite ends of the same things. To find balance, you should experience both. On the earthly plane, you can physically see the differences in polarity. A coin has both a back and a front, trees can be tall or short, you can go in or out a door, there's hot and cold, windy and still, loud and quiet, happy and sad, and the list can go on and on. When you physically see these opposites they're easier to understand. You know if someone is angry to leave them alone until they find their balance and are peaceful again.

Let's say you're a person who prefers staying in your house and isn't very social. Later, in your current lifetime or in the next one, in order to experience soul growth, you'll need to experience the opposite lifestyle where you are very social and hardly ever stay at home. Maybe you're currently barely making ends meet. According to the Law of Balance and Polarity, you'll need to also experience financial wealth. Money is tricky, however—if you manage it correctly, you can enjoy having the monetary wealth you desire without losing it through frivolous spending. Have you ever gotten paid and then gone out on Friday night and blown your whole paycheck? Most people don't do this because they have bills to pay if they want to keep a roof over their heads, but it's a prime example of the Law of Balance and Polarity. When you get paid you're on the plus side of the money scale and you've got money for the rent, groceries, gas, and everything else you need until the next payday but if you blow all your money in one night of going out, you're on the opposite end of the scale and are broke until your next payday. This is a hard lesson to learn but by experiencing both ends of the spectrum, you will be able to find balance.

When you experience adversity in life, there is always an opposite pole to that adversity. If you find yourself getting lost in thinking about the problematic situation you're in, expand your vision to look at the other side of the spectrum for the great things that are there. You may find yourself in the middle of a thunderstorm, but there will always be clear weather when it passes. Your thoughts about the situation will make it positive or negative. During difficult times it's easy to look at things negatively, but if you catch yourself doing this, changing your perspective enables you to see the positive. Think of it as putting yourself in someone else's shoes. To you, a rainy day may be miserable but to someone else whose garden needs rain, it's wonderful. Learning to look at every situation from different perspectives allows you to see the extreme opposites and find the point of balance between them. It is also a Divine connection that allows soul growth.

There Are Two Sides to Every Situation

Understanding that there are two sides to everything is a life lesson for most of us. You can't see how going to extremes affects you. This means that to become balanced, you must first experience being out of balance. Everyone has a polarity within themselves. As spiritual beings, it is our job to understand these conflicting opposites inside us and find a way to bring balance to them.

Have you ever been asked if you're right-brained or left-brained? Research shows that right brained people tend to be more imaginative, passionate, intuitive and creative. They are often interested in the arts and music, are very touchy-feely, easily use nonverbal communication, and enjoy daydreaming and creative visualization. Left brained people tend to be analytical, logical, think in words, want just the facts, enjoy math, think in a linear or sequencing way, and computation. And guess what? Everyone has both inside us! So how do you find balance between your left brain and your right brain? You use a little of both. For example, I'm very intuitive but balance my intuition by always looking for a logical reason for something before I decide that it is in fact intuition or of a paranormal nature.

Once you are in balance internally it raises your frequency, connects you more fully with the Divine, and is reflected in your reality. You'll get along with others better, be happier, and more content with your life. Balance allows you to feel harmony within yourself so that when you are faced with difficult circumstances, you're able to see it from different perspectives instead of only the negative extreme. Becoming balanced internally makes it easier to find balance in your daily activities. Things that once aggravated you are no longer as negative as they were because you can see a purpose in their existence. Balance allows you to feel a deeper connection to the Divine and feel connected to the whole of the universe. When you're in balance you no longer tend to go to either extreme of a spectrum. You're able to keep your emotions centered and learn from your experiences. Negative things can actually turn into great things.

While you're finding balance in situations by not going to extremes and becoming balanced internally at a spiritual level, it's important to remember to be balanced in your daily activities as well. If you've got so much to do that you never have any time to just relax, you're on the extreme side of the to-do spectrum. If this is the case, schedule time for fun, rest, and relaxation, and then make sure you actually do it. If you're going full steam ahead all the time, you'll eventually burn out from exhaustion. The polarity of this would be if you never did anything and were bored to tears all the time from watching too much television or sitting around doing nothing. If that's you, create a goal and then take the necessary steps to achieve it.

Do Something

The Law of Balance and Polarity means avoiding spending a lot of time reflecting on situations to the point where you forget to go out and do things. You have to experience life so you can find balance in all things. Sheltering yourself away from others creates a lack of experiences that can help you gain and maintain steadiness and stability, the balance needed to connect to your spiritual self and the world around you.

Living the Law of Balance and Polarity is like all the other universal laws in that it is an ongoing commitment to personal and spiritual growth so you can achieve all you desire during this lifetime on the earthly plane of existence. Consider it a lifestyle change. If you want to become fit, you make a lifestyle change to eat better and exercise more, right? Once you get used to eating differently and working out you stop thinking about it as much. Making a lifestyle change by living universal laws helps you to bring your spiritual energy into balance. It works the same way.

Try It Now

The next time you find yourself in an adverse situation, you can find your balance quickly by doing this exercise. Regardless of the situation, take a step back out of the chaos and find a place to sit down. Close your eyes and take a few deep breaths. With each inhale imagine calmness and positivity flowing inside you and with each exhale imagine the negativity of the situation leaving you. Once you feel as if you've found your balance open your eyes. Think of the opposite of the situation at hand and look at it from that perspective. How can you turn this negative into a positive? Once you have a solution, you can return to the situation and resolve it.

Practical Application Tips

- Make time in your day for the things that bring you joy.

- Avoid material distractions.

- Find balance within to find success without.

- Let go of extreme behavior.

- Look at situations from a different perspective to find balance.

- Balance raises your frequency, resulting in positivity, happiness, and success.

- You're not right brained or left brained when you're in balance.

- Keep your emotions centered.

- Make decisions, don't ride the fence. When you are for something you're also against something on the same spectrum. Everything has an opposite, when you can see it, understand it, then you can balance it.

See Also Chapter 26: The Law of Attachment and Detachment

39

THE LAW OF SUPPLY AND DEMAND

— 🕊 —

Today I will be precise in my universal requests
and aware of the supply delivered in response.

THE LAW OF SUPPLY and Demand states that for every demand, the universe will provide the supply to meet that demand; however, without a demand there will be no supply. In other words, if there is a need for something, it will be provided. This law is set in motion when the demand for something arises.

In the physical world, the Law of Supply and Demand states the price of a product or service is based on the demand for that service. This was first noted by Aristotle in *Politics Book 1* part 2 when he discusses the practical part of "wealth-getting" and the story of Thales the Milesian who gave deposits on all the olive presses because he believed there would be an abundance of olives. Then, he rented out the olive presses to others and made money. The Law of Supply and Demand says that the higher the demand, or if the supply is limited, the higher the price will be. Supply provides us with the products we demand in our daily lives.

The universe works in the same way. When you request something from it, the universe is happy to supply you with what you requested. Trust in the universe to deliver what you requested and believe you'll receive it. Ask for what you want and expect it to come to you. If you want it, it will be given, but you will have to work for it too. When you go to the grocery store you don't just teleport there and back (but wouldn't that be fun?), you have to get in your car, hire a taxi, ride your bike or walk to the store, pick out all of your food and drinks, bring it all home, then store it in the refrigerator and cabinets. I recently saw an inspirational graphic online that said something like "Do what you love and the money will follow," then it lists a bunch of things like eating pizza and then says "Now I wait." I know this is meant to be funny, but it shows the missing link in many people's mindsets: we must take active steps to work toward goals, not just sit back and wait for them to manifest while doing things that aren't geared toward their appearance in our lives.

Make a Request, Not a Demand

Notice that I'm not using the word *demand* when discussing asking the universe for assistance. Demanding instead of requesting what you want implies a feeling that is deserving and entitled, like you must have your way. This attitude can actually keep you from obtaining what you want. Be firm in your request so there is no doubt as to what you need and want to receive. When you ask with firmness, respect, and gratitude, you align yourself with the abundance of the universe and you'll achieve faster results. Just keep this in mind when making requests for abundance.

In life, we must always study and learn in order to be aware of what is happening in our world, the progress being made, and how life is happening within the human race. If there's something you want, you must become more aware of how it works. If you want to become a doctor, you'll have to know which classes to take, how internships work, and what you'll do after you have your degree. You can't become a doctor until you're aware of the steps you need to take to obtain a medical degree. Then you must have the drive and desire to take those classes and do internships as well as anything else required of you to become a doctor. That way, when the universe supplies you with the opportunity, for example, acceptance into medical school, you're aware of what you need to do to bring your dream to fruition.

Let's look at how the universe delivers the supply for your requests. Many times the universe will offer you the path to your request by putting you in a situation where you can become successful or giving you an opportunity or a brilliant idea that will lead to what you want. Have you ever had an idea you never acted on and then down the road it was the most successful thing in the world? I remember in my early twenties, I came up with a great idea for a new type of hair bow that molded against the back of your head and held your hair out of the way. About a year and a half after I had this idea, the banana clip was the hottest trend of the 1980s. It was exactly the same thing I'd thought of, but since I didn't act on it, the opportunity was given to someone else who did. So if you receive an idea, do everything you can to act upon what the universe supplied to you and bring it to fruition. There's a saying in business that opportunity doesn't knock twice, and it's true—if you take action, you may just become financially wealthy along the way.

After you ask the universe for what you want, release the thought and let it travel to do what it's supposed to do. Give it time to be delivered. What if, in your job, you were allowed no flexibility to complete tasks in the time it took you to do them? If your boss said he wanted you to have X report on his desk by 2:00 pm, Y report by 2:06, and Z report by 2:10, and the current time is 1:55 pm, you'd think he was nuts, wouldn't you? That's not enough time to start thinking about what you're going to put in the three reports. Getting them delivered by those times is *not* going to happen. When you put overly strict limitations on your requests such as time, the location, and the means, you're probably not going to achieve what you want. You're interrupting the flow of the delivery from the universal supply because you're being way too specific in what you want. That said, it's okay to be specific … just not overly specific. If you want a boyfriend or a girlfriend, don't say, *"I want a boyfriend/girlfriend,"* instead say, *"I want a boyfriend/girlfriend who isn't in a relationship with anyone else."* Otherwise, you just may find yourself with a problem you didn't want on your hands if you don't know the other person is already involved with someone else when you two get involved. Likewise, it wouldn't be productive to say, *"I want a boyfriend/ girlfriend who isn't in a relationship with anyone else whom I will meet at the pizza shop on 4th Avenue at 10 pm on Wednesday of next week and who is tall and will have brown hair, green eyes, straight teeth, and a wonderful smile."* Wow! Asking for much? That's the kind of over-specification that you don't want to include in your request.

When problems arise, you can eliminate them by requesting that the universe remove the problem and deliver the opposite. If you're having problems in your relationship, ask that you are clear in your speech and the other person correctly understands your intention. Ask that problematic situations leave you. Otherwise, they may hang around.

In our physical reality, when there is a shortage of something, people providing that something will often blame someone else when supplies are lean. For example, if there's a shortage of tomatoes, the grocery store managers might say the distributors aren't getting enough tomatoes to stores, and the distributors might say the farmers are to blame for the shortage of tomatoes this year. They didn't plant enough! In fact, maybe they *did* plant enough and the plants were eaten by some bug or there was a drought and not enough water for the tomato plants to survive. It's important not to blame others but state facts. When you're requesting something from the universe, it's not the universe's fault if you don't see the opportunity it has delivered to you or if you do recognize it and chose not to take advantage of it. Instead of playing the blame game, be consciously aware of your choices and decisions when supply is offered to you.

Just like you can change the world's supply and demand through your buying choices, you can also change the way the universe supplies what you need in your life. You deserve everything you desire and the universe will supply it to you when you ask. Remember you have to ask to receive. Asking can change your life for the better in ways you may not have expected when you made the request. Ask, receive, be thankful, and enjoy.

Try It Now

Take a minute to think about your attitude and how you ask for things from the universe. Are you half-heartedly asking for something one time and then giving up on it because you don't believe it will come? Are you asking with a lack mentality or an abundance one? Are you being specific or vague in your request? You've put the request out there and now you're just waiting for it to arrive while doing any work you can to help it get to you. Now, think of something that you want or need. Carefully phrase it, and then ask the universe for it. The universe, working through the Law of Supply and Demand will deliver what you need.

Practical Application Tips

- Ask for what you need.

- Be thankful for what you receive.

- Remain aware in order to know when your universal delivery arrives.

- Remove limitations. Abundance is infinite and you can have all you want.

- Give the universe time to work.

- Don't give so many specifications within your requests that you make it impossible for the universe to meet them all.

- Remember the universe works on its own time frame and will deliver your request when you're ready for it and not before.

- Act on any ideas you receive from the universe that could lead to success.

- Be firm in your requests but not demanding with a negative attitude.

- Eliminate problems through universal requests for removal and delivery of the opposite.

See Also Chapter 31: The Law of Allowing

40

THE LAW OF POTENTIAL

— 🕊 —

*I will choose to be all I can be, achieve all I can
achieve, and make the most of my potential.*

THE LAW OF POTENTIAL states that there is an unlimited amount of
possibilities and infinite potential within everyone and everything in the
universe due to the connection of energy to universal consciousness. Potential means having the capacity or ability to develop into something
that can be useful to yourself or others in the future. It exists in possibility until you take action to achieve it. Aristotle described potentiality as
the fulfillment of a possibility as brought about by actuality. Our spiritual
beings are pure energy that is part of the universal consciousness. As we
are part of the whole, which offers unlimited abundance, than we too are
part of that abundance. This means there is nothing that can hold us back
from achieving what we want. With no limits on what you can achieve,

what you can be, how you can serve others, and the things you can gain in your life, what will you do? That's a million-dollar question, isn't it? If you can do anything because there are no restrictions holding you back, what would you choose? Understanding you are pure potential and that you can reach any goal you want really alters your perspective on life. You can send and receive your energy to the universe to manifest anything because as a spiritual being with an energetic frequency, you *are* energy. So what will it be? What do you want out of life?

Your Choices Are Important

Living the Law of Potential means every choice you make will affect you as a spiritual being, including your purpose and the plans you've made to achieve your desires. To fully come into your own potential, you must maintain control over your spiritual self and your frequency. When you take control and form the energy of your inner self in order to achieve your highest potential, you'll experience more joy. Until you try to achieve your desires you're not going to know just how much you are capable of doing. You may be the world's greatest computer genius, but until you learn about computers and work with them to understand them inside and out, you're not going to know that about yourself. When you cooperate with universal consciousness, you can do more than you ever thought possible. Unveil the potential within you.

To begin, you must start at the beginning. Make a conscious decision to live up to your capabilities. There aren't any shortcuts to developing your fullest potential. When you try to take shortcuts, you're cheating yourself out of gaining valuable knowledge that could be beneficial in the future. Take your time; develop every aspect of your potential until it's bursting at the seams and it leaves you with a sense of fulfillment and pride in your accomplishment. Read as much as you can about every subject that interests you. The Internet is chock-full of information that can enlighten and inform you. You can also listen to live webinars, podcasts, or radio shows online. Those are always fun and you could even call in with your questions. The more knowledge you have, the easier it will be to reach your potential. Focus and attention are also important qualities that allow you to clearly see the path before you, leading you to fulfill the greatness within you. All you have to do is walk the path. If you need to take little tiny steps at first, do it. Even babies must learn how to walk. Soon you'll grow by leaps and bounds and maybe have a hard time keeping up with yourself.

Be proud of every accomplishment you make along the way. By giving each little step importance, you're praising yourself. This helps your confidence grow and gives you a power boost to continue on towards the ultimate end goal. Make sure you maintain your focus on the goal. It's often easy to get distracted and lose sight of what we really want. If you get distracted for too long, you may forget about the goal you wanted to reach—out of sight, out of mind! Remain on task to achieve success.

Think back to what you wanted to be when you grew up. I wanted to be a veterinarian but had a very difficult time with math. I also wanted to be an oceanographer, but I have bad sinuses and can't dive. It wouldn't be right of me to blame my not becoming a vet or oceanographer on my math skills or sinuses. I must accept that I wasn't willing to put in the effort required to understand the math, and I could have always worked an office type of oceanographer job but that just didn't have the same appeal. For a while I wasn't sure what I wanted to do for work but once I made a decision, I went for the goal. I've had several careers since that time, which gave me a well-rounded knowledge of people, spirituality and the world, which have proven invaluable to me as a writer. My spiritual self always knew I'd ultimately be a writer but I needed all those other experiences to be successful at it. If you still desire the career you fantasized about as a kid, it's never too late to try for it. You can achieve any goal you've set for yourself if you work toward it. If you've always wanted to be a singer, sing. It would be sad to regret something in your life simply because you didn't attempt to live up to your potential.

Be Exceptional

Don't be average, be exceptional! Take a look at the people around you. How many of them are being truly exceptional by striving to reach their potential? The number is probably less than you would have originally thought. Being exceptional requires commitment to your desires. It means you're willing to work harder, give up more of your time and energy, and always see things through to the end. Not everyone is willing to do that. When they're not willing, they can't live up to the potential inside of themselves. While most people who are living the Law of Potential tend to be independent thinkers who don't like to follow the majority, not everyone has the desire to be out there front and center. There are plenty of people who live up to their potential without getting into the limelight. Walking the path makes you feel as if you've made great accomplishments, you're doing all you can, and you're happy with your progress. You're the only one who can decide which path will enable you to reach your true potential.

Sometimes you'll have different or multiple pathways to fulfilling your potential. I'm happy being a writer because it enables me to teach on a larger scale. I'm also happy raising horses because I've always had a deep connection to animals, especially horses. I feel both these careers allow me to fulfill my potential in different ways. The Law of Potential does not limit you to any one career, hobby, or life path. Remember that there is infinite potential within each one of us. There are no limits to what you can do or achieve except the limits you place on yourself.

To define areas where you can reach your potential, look at the things you like to do. Are you a great cook? Maybe you could write recipe books. If you enjoy sports, you could become a coach or sports announcer. If you enjoy puzzles and figuring things out, you might be an awesome detective. By examining the things that bring you joy, you can determine ways to excel in those areas. Think about how the area you select will affect you as a person. Will it enable you to reach a level of fame where everyone knows your name? Are you ready for that kind of celebrity? What will you attain on a personal level once you reach your potential? Being of service to others is often a driving force for many people. Helping, teaching, and supporting causes that help others also helps you develop your potential. Living a fulfilled life doesn't often equate with great riches or celebrity status. It can be as simple as lending a helping hand to a neighbor. If you aspire to greatness, know there isn't anything stopping you from living up to your potential and reaching for the stars. Go for what you want because the universe's infinite potential is ready and willing to help you achieve anything you desire.

Try It Now

The next time you're at the store, grab a composition book or any small blank journal. Every time you have a minor success write it down in the journal and include how it made you feel to make the achievement. It could be as minor as finding a parking space close to the elevator instead of having to walk across the whole parking lot. Or it can be as complicated as something positive happening in a relationship. Writing these things down allows you to look back at them when you're feeling like things aren't moving forward like they should. Journaling is a great way to express yourself, make notes of progress, and get your feelings out and down on paper. You never have to show this journal to anyone else. It's only for you to keep you moving forward and pump you up when you're feeling down.

Practical Application Tips

- Give importance to every success you achieve.

- Past desires can be fulfilled today.

- Do your best to live a life without regret by living up to your potential.

- The potential of the universe is unlimited. You can do, be, and achieve anything you want.

- There isn't just one path to potential. You may experience many ways to reach fulfillment.

- Only you can decide if you're willing to reach your potential.

- If it's easy, everyone would do it. (What a great saying; it's so true!)

- Your possibilities are endless. Try them all.

- Keep a journal of your successes to gain a power boost when things aren't going as planned.

See Also Chapter 3: The Law of Gratitude

Conclusion

Now that you've learned about forty of the universal laws, it's time to put them into action. Try the exercises, alter them to fit your needs, or create your own. Universal laws will always bring you success if you apply them to your life.

Being successful incorporates many things that you will be required to do along the path. You'll need to stay positive. Being optimistic, even during difficult times, gives you the power to make things better in your life. Don't give all your attention to the things that go wrong because then you'll just put yourself into a pattern of negativity which can block your success. Everyone who has ever wanted to achieve something sets themselves to specific standards. If you fail to meet those standards, you may consider yourself a failure. Don't. Everyone has moments when things don't go according to plan, and it will not last. Remember the saying: This too shall pass. Failures are only temporary setbacks on the long-term path of success. In order to succeed, begin and try.

Being truly successful means achieving what you want while understanding, respecting, and empathizing with those you meet along the way. Everyone has dreams they want to achieve, and everyone experiences problems sometimes. When you see people as the spiritual beings they are, you honor their truth, respect their desires, act with compassion, and identify with them. We are all the same inside—Divine spiritual beings filled with love and light. When you can connect with others on these levels, you have achieved more success than any material possession can give you. Sure, having a nice house and car, plenty of money, and lots of fancy toys are signs that you've been successful in your career and are financially well off, but things are just that—things. It's how you grow spiritually and the lessons you learn while on the earthly plane of existence that matter most. Financial success is something everyone would like to enjoy because it makes life on the earthly plane easier. Just don't let it be the only type of success you strive to achieve in this lifetime.

You'll also be required to ask for and receive help as you practice living in accordance with universal laws. You can't go it alone; you're not supposed to. Connecting and interacting with others is a major part of growth. Most of all, it's important to keep your life in perspective. You know what success means to you and what you'd like to achieve in this lifetime. On a soul level, only you know the path and lessons you chose prior to birth. It doesn't matter what other people think; they can't live your life for you. Change what you can, and if something can't be changed, deal with it as it is.

Living on the earthly plane is exciting, wonderful, and a great way to become more in tune with our true spiritual natures. It's a way to learn and grow. The universe is there to help us every step of the way if we'll only let it by cooperating through the implementation of spiritual laws in our lives. Success comes from the desire inside you. It's not based on your circumstances, family, or anything else. The energy within you can create all you desire. It can shift negativity to positivity and manifest anything you want … and that's the key. You must want it, be willing to work for it, and trust in the universal laws to deliver it. You are successful. You are Spirit. You are Divine.

Bibliography

Alvarez, Melissa. *Simply Give Thanks: A Beginner's Guide to Joyful Living through the Power of Spiritual Gratitude.* North Palm Beach, FL: Adrema Press, 2013.

———. *365 Ways to Raise Your Frequency: Simple Tools to Increase Your Spiritual Energy for Balance, Purpose, and Joy.* Woodbury, MN: Llewellyn Worldwide, 2012.

Anapol, Deborah Taj. *The Seven Natural Laws of Love.* Santa Rosa, CA: Elite Books, 2005.

Angelheart, Anne E. *Twelve Universal Laws: The Truth That Will Transform Your Life.* Bloomington, IN: Balboa Press, 2011.

Aristotle. *On the Soul*, part 5, book III. Translated by J. A. Smith. Internet Classics Archive, classics.mit.edu/Aristotle/soul.3.iii.html.

———. *Politics*, part 2, book I. Translated by Benjamin Jowett. Internet Classics Archive, classics.mit.edu/Aristotle/politics.1.one.html.

Barnum, Melanie. *The Steady Way to Greatness: Liberate Your Intuitive Potential & Manifest Your Heartfelt Desires.* Woodbury, MN: Llewellyn Worldwide, 2014.

Bernhard, Franz. *Udānavarga*, section 5:18. Gottingen, Germany: Vandenhoek & Ruprecht, 1965. At www.ancient-buddhist-texts .net/Buddhist-Texts/S1-Udanavarga/index.htm.

Biceaga, Victor. *The Concept of Passivity in Husserl's Phenomenology.* New York: Springer Science & Business Media B.V., 2010.

Carnegie, Dale. *How to Stop Worrying and Start Living.* New York: Pocket Books, 2010.

Chopra, Deepak. *The Seven Spiritual Laws of Success: A Pocketbook Guide to Fulfilling Your Dreams.* San Rafael, CA: Amber-Allen Publishing and Novato, CA: New World Library, 1994.

Conwell, Russell H. *Acres of Diamonds.* Amazon Digital Services Kindle Edition, 2011.

Cooper, Diana. *A Little Light on the Spiritual Laws.* Scotland, UK: Findhorn Press, 2007.

Cooper, Marianna M. *The Aha! Factor: How to Use Your Intuition to Get What You Desire and Deserve.* London: Watkins Publishing, 2016.

Danaher, James P., PhD. "The Laws of Thought." In *The Philosopher,* volume XCII, no. 1, Spring 2004.

Descartes, René. *Meditations on First Philosophy.* Internet Encyclopedia of Philosophy. Translated by Elizabeth S. Haldane. selfpace.uconn .edu/class/percep/DescartesMeditations.pdf 1996.

Dotts, Richard. *Banned Manifestation Secrets of Ancient Spiritual Masters.* Kindle edition, 2014.

Drummond, Henry. *Natural Law in the Spiritual World.* New York: Hurst & Company, 2012.

Gilbert, Elizabeth. *Big Magic: Creative Living Beyond Fear.* New York: Riverhead Books, 2015.

Goldsmith, Marshall. *What Got You Here Won't Get You There.* New York: Hyperion Books, 2007.

Hatch, Wendell Calvin. *The Second Golden Rule.* Bloomington, IN: WestBow Press, 2012.

Heckert, Paul A. *Physics 101 Tutorials: Understanding Newton's Laws of Motion and Gravity.* Kindle edition, 2011.

Hill, Napoleon, *Think and Grow Rich.* Kindle edition, 2015.

Langland, William. *The Vision of Piers Plowman,* 1360–1387. Oxford Text Archive at quod.lib.umich.edu/cgi/t/text/text -idx?c=cme;idno=PPlLan.

Laster, Robert Lee. *100 Universal Laws, Cosmic Order.* Kindle edition, 2015.

Longmore, Jennifer. *88 Universal Laws.* Kindle edition, 2014.

Michael, Edward Salim. *The Law of Attention Nada Yoga and the Way of Inner Vigilance.* Rochester, VT: Inner Traditions, 2010.

O'Neill, Jennifer. *Universal Laws: 18 Powerful Laws & The Secret Behind Manifesting Your Desires.* Kailua, HI: Limitless Publishing, 2013.

Parker, Sybil P. *McGraw-Hill Concise Encyclopedia of Science & Technology Third Edition.* New York: McGraw-Hill, 1992.

Perry, Justin. *I Wish I Knew This 20 Years Ago … : Understanding the Universal Laws That Govern All Things.* Kindle edition, 2014.

Randazzo, Dottie. *442 Cosmic & Universal Laws.* Kindle Edition, 2011.

Schwartz, David J. *The Magic of Thinking Big*. New York: Prentice Hall Press, 2014.

Sivananda, Sri Swami. *Thought Power*. Himalayas, India: Divine Life Society, 2013.

The Holy Bible, King James Version: Romans 3:27, Luke 6:31, Genesis 11:5, 6. New York: American Bible Society, 1999.

Three Initiates. *The Kybalion: A Study of The Hermetic Philosophy of Ancient Egypt and Greece*. Chicago, IL: The Yogi Publication Society Masonic Temple, 1912.

Tracy, Brian. *The Universal Laws of Success and Achievement*. Wheeling, IL: Nightingale-Conant, 2014.

Tzu, Lao. *Tao Teh King*. Translated by James Legge. Oxford, UK: Clarendon Press, 1891.

Vitale, Joe. *The Prosperity Factor: How to Achieve Unlimited Wealth in Every Area of Your Life*. Blaine, WA: Expert Author Publishing, 2016.

Wattles, Wallace D. *Wallace D. Wattles Master Collection: 84 Rare Books and Articles by Wallace D. Wattles, Author of The Science of Getting Rich*. Kindle edition, 2016.

Weschcke, Carl Llewellyn, and Joe H. Slate. *Self-Empowerment and Your Subconscious Mind: Your Unlimited Resource for Health, Success, Long Life & Spiritual Attainment*. Woodbury, MN: Llewellyn Worldwide, 2010.

Wilson, Elisabeth. *The Feel Good Factory On Stress-Free Living: Calm-Spreading, Mind-Soothing, Strain-Slaying Ideas for a Happy Life*. The Feel Good Factory, Kindle edition, 2009.

Wojton, Djuna. *Karmic Choices: How Making the Right Decisions Can Create Enduring Joy*. Woodbury, MN: Llewellyn Worldwide, 2014.

To Write to the Author

If you wish to contact the author or would like more information about this book, please write to the author in care of Llewellyn Worldwide, and we will forward your request. Both the author and the publisher appreciate hearing from you and learning of your enjoyment of this book and how it has helped you. Llewellyn Worldwide cannot guarantee that every letter written to the author can be answered, but all will be forwarded. Please write to:

Melissa Alvarez
℅ Llewellyn Worldwide
2143 Wooddale Drive
Woodbury, MN 55125-2989

Please enclose a self-addressed stamped envelope for reply,
or $1.00 to cover costs. If outside the USA, enclose
an international postal reply coupon.

Many of Llewellyn's authors have websites with additional information and resources. For more information, please visit www.llewellyn.com.

GET MORE AT LLEWELLYN.COM

Visit us online to browse hundreds of our books and decks, plus sign up to receive our e-newsletters and exclusive online offers.

- Free tarot readings • Spell-a-Day • Moon phases
- Recipes, spells, and tips • Blogs • Encyclopedia
- Author interviews, articles, and upcoming events

GET SOCIAL WITH LLEWELLYN

Find us on   🐦 @LlewellynBooks

www.Facebook.com/LlewellynBooks

GET BOOKS AT LLEWELLYN

LLEWELLYN ORDERING INFORMATION

 Order online: Visit our website at www.llewellyn.com to select your books and place an order on our secure server.

Order by phone:
- Call toll free within the U.S. at 1-877-NEW-WRLD (1-877-639-9753)
- Call toll free within Canada at 1-866-NEW-WRLD (1-866-639-9753)
- We accept VISA, MasterCard, American Express and Discover

Order by mail:
Send the full price of your order (MN residents add 6.875% sales tax) in U.S. funds, plus postage and handling to: Llewellyn Worldwide, 2143 Wooddale Drive Woodbury, MN 55125-2989

POSTAGE AND HANDLING

STANDARD (U.S. & Canada):
(Please allow 12 business days)
$30.00 and under, add $4.00.
$30.01 and over, FREE SHIPPING.

INTERNATIONAL ORDERS:
$16.00 for one book, plus $3.00 for each additional book.

Visit us online for more shipping options. Prices subject to change.

FREE CATALOG!

To order, call 1-877-NEW-WRLD ext. 8236 or visit our website

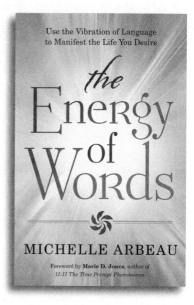

Use the Vibration of Language
to Manifest the Life You Desire

the
Energy
of
Words

MICHELLE ARBEAU

Foreword by **Marie D. Jones**, author of
11:11 The Time Prompt Phenomenon

The Energy of Words

Use the Vibration of Language to Manifest the Life You Desire
MICHELLE ARBEAU

Manifest the life you truly desire with *The Energy of Words*. Choose the most powerful words and let the secret energy of language attract joy and abundance into your life!

Join internationally renowned numerologist Michelle Arbeau as she shows you how to determine your top ten power words; how to calculate the vibration of a word through the language of numbers; practical tips for positivity; the top one hundred positive and negative words; and stories of celebrities who have successfully worked with the power of words.

Negative words are energetic junk food. We can't manifest our desires if we're using words of lack and doubt. Learn how to eliminate negative vocabulary and replace it with positive personalized language that will transform your life into one of fulfillment and gratitude.

978-0-7387-3664-8, 312 pp., 5³⁄₁₆ x 8   **$15.99**

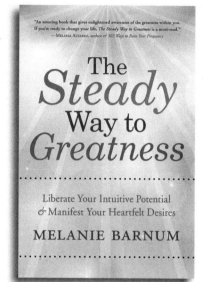

"An amazing book that gives enlightened awareness of the greatness within you.
If you're ready to change your life, *The Steady Way to Greatness* is a must-read."
—MELISSA ALVAREZ, author of *365 Ways to Raise Your Frequency*

The
Steady
Way to
Greatness

Liberate Your Intuitive Potential
& Manifest Your Heartfelt Desires

MELANIE BARNUM

The Steady Way to Greatness
Liberate Your Intuitive Potential & Manifest Your Heartfelt Desires
Melanie Barnum

Use intuition and psychic development to master the law of attraction and manifest the life you truly desire. *The Steady Way to Greatness* is a new and groundbreaking combination of manifestation and intuition for success in career, finances, love, relationships, spirituality, and more. Organized into a progression of fifty-two weekly practices, this guide includes affirmations and other exercises designed to increase confidence, discover the power of goal setting, and expose the magnificence that resides within.

Intuitive counselor Melanie Barnum is the perfect guide to help you reach your true potential. The stories and exercises she includes are designed for:

- Exploring positive and negative attitudes
- Opening to intuitive senses
- Identifying strengths
- Creating and living your dream life

978-0-7387-3835-2, 264 pp., 6 x 9   **$15.99**

To order, call 1-877-NEW-WRLD
Prices subject to change without notice
Order at Llewellyn.com 24 hours a day, 7 days a week!